Energize Your Meetings
WiTH LAUGHTER

Sheila Feigelson

ASCD

Association for Supervision and Curriculum Development
Alexandria, Virginia USA

Association for Supervision and Curriculum Development
1703 N. Beauregard St. • Alexandria, VA 22311-1714 USA
Telephone: 1-800-933-2723 or 703-578-9600 • Fax: 703-575-5400
Web site: http://www.ascd.org • E-mail: member@ascd.org

Gene R. Carter, *Executive Director*
Michelle Terry, *Associate Executive Director, Program Development*
Nancy Modrak, *Director, Publishing*
John O'Neil, *Acquisitions Director*
Julie Houtz, *Managing Editor of Books*
Carolyn R. Pool, *Associate Editor*
René Bahrenfuss, *Copy Editor*
Charles D. Halverson, *Project Assistant*

Gary Bloom, *Director, Design and Production Services*
Karen Monaco, *Senior Designer*
Tracey A. Smith, *Production Manager*
Dina Murray, *Production Coordinator*
John Franklin, *Production Coordinator*
Cynthia Stock, *Desktop Publisher*
Winfield Swanson, *Indexer*

Copyright © 1998 by Sheila Feigelson, P.O. Box 7262, Ann Arbor, MI 48107 USA. **Readers are encouraged to use or adapt materials in Figures 4.3, 4.4, 4.5, 8.1, 10.1, and the Appendixes for noncommercial use; permission is not needed for such use.** No other part of this publication may be reproduced or transmitted in any form or by any means, electronic or mechanical, including photocopy, recording, or any information storage and retrieval system, without written permission from Sheila Feigelson. Readers who wish to duplicate material copyrighted by the author should contact her at the address above or by e-mail (HappyF@aol.com). Any duplicated material from this book must cite the source and include a copyright notice (e.g., copyright (c)1998 by Sheila Feigelson).

Permission to duplicate materials copyrighted by others must be obtained from the copyright holders, as follows: Figures 4.1, 4.2, and 7.1–7.4: Droodles by Roger Price reprinted by permission of Price Stern Sloan, Inc. from *Classic Droodles*, copyright 1953, (c) 1981 by Roger Price. Address requests to Permissions Editor, The Putnam & Grosset Group, Price Stern Sloan, Inc., 200 Madison Avenue, New York, NY 10016 USA. Figures 6.1–6.3, 7.5, 10.2, and 12.1: Potshots copyright (various dates) by Ashleigh Brilliant, Brilliant Enterprises, 117 W. Valerio Street, Santa Barbara, CA 93101 USA. Excerpts by Robert Pike in Chapters 4 and 5: (c) Robert W. Pike. All rights reserved. Phone: 800-383-9210 or 612-829-1954. World Wide Web: http://www.cttbobpike.com.

ASCD publications present a variety of viewpoints. The views expressed or implied in this book should not be interpreted as official positions of the Association.

Printed in the United States of America.

s12/98

ASCD Stock No.: 198055
ASCD member price: $10.95   nonmember price: $13.95

Library of Congress Cataloging-in-Publication Data

Feigelson, Sheila, 1940–
     Energize your meetings with laughter / Sheila Feigelson.
     p. cm.
   Includes bibliographical references.
   ISBN 0-87120-315-4 (pbk.)
   1. Meetings—Planning. 2. Teachers' institutes—Planning. 3. Wit and humor. 4. Laughter. 5. Humor in the workplace (Personnel Management) I. Title.
   LB1751 .F36 1998
   658.4'56—dc21   98-40161
                                                         CIP

06 05 04 03 02 01   10 9 8 7 6 5 4 3 2

*Energize
Your
Meetings
with
Laughter*

Dedicated to my father,
H. D. (Hy) Berman,
from whom I've learned
the meaning of being Happy.

January 12, 1998

Acknowledgments

I grew up in a family that values humor. At an early age I became aware of its power to help me make friends and to communicate serious messages. And I am grateful for that.

Though it is not always easy to know just where an idea originated, we often know who brought the idea to our awareness. It was Joel Goodman who taught me the difference between being serious and being solemn about the subject of humor. You can have fun and still be serious; but you can't have much fun and be solemn at the same time. He was the first person I ever heard discuss that idea. As founder and director of The Humor Project in Saratoga Springs, New York, Joel's work in humor and creativity has affected thousands of people. I am grateful to be one of them. I thank him for his first invitation to speak at the International Conference on the Positive Power of Humor and Creativity in 1991; this opportunity prompted me to gather my thoughts about humor and meetings. This book is an outgrowth of that initial presentation.

Over the years, I've developed a vast collection of ideas, quotes, activities, and examples of putting humor to work in classrooms, meetings, work settings and everyday life. Many of them would still be in my head, file folders, and boxes were it not for the encouragement and help of many wonderful people.

For their help in getting my thoughts into book form, I especially thank the following people:

☺ Pat Materka, who astounds me by her ability to turn even the most drab, ho-hum sentence into a colorful and breezy one. As initial editor and writing coach, supporter and friend, her influencing hand is felt in this book (if not in *this* sentence).

☺ Geraldine Markel, my long-time dear friend, colleague, and mentor all rolled into one, for reading the various versions of the manuscript and offering insightful comments about content and style. Her ability to make a person feel like a million bucks even as she offers suggestions for improvement is among her treasured gifts to me. She has been a true cheerleader.

☺ Judy Goldfein, my sister the editor, for always being available to listen and laugh on the phone with me, and to use her professional skills to help me not use so many words to express my ideas with (!).

☺ David Berman, my brother the physicist, who, from the beginning, wondered how I was really going to write a book and is no doubt shaking his head in amazement that—yes!—I actually *did* it.

☺ Hy (H. D.) Berman, my 89-year-old father, who, from the very start, read parts of the book and encouraged me to "hurry up and finish" so that he could go out and buy his copy. I am grateful for the reassurance he has given me my whole life with his often-used expression, "That's a good idea." Had my mother, Ruth, lived to see this book, I know she, too, would have loved the idea, as well as the contents.

☺ Randy Milgram, the editor who, among other things, helped me realize that exclamation points are often overused!!!

☺ Sarah Wood, the editor who snapped me out of my writing funk and taught me the word "sobriquet."

☺ Nancy Modrak, John O'Neil, Julie Houtz, Carolyn Pool, and René Bahrenfuss, the ASCD group of editors who helped structure and refine the presentation of materials. I appreciate their talents, collegial work styles, and prompt, reassuring responses to all my questions.

☺ David Aberdeen, Harlene Appelman, Lael Berman Gerding, Warren Cohen, Zonya Foco, Penny Griffith, Sylvia Gordon, Sandy Goldberg, Sylvia Hacker, Christeen Holdwick, Allen Klein, Tony Putnam, Gay Rosenwald, Karen Roth, Dotty Lou Sarff, Donna Winkelman, and Phyllis Werbel—friends and colleagues who have played a significant role by either reading portions of the book or helping to clarify some thoughts, by talking about it or providing some examples, or by just listening to me ramble on.

☺ Lou, my one and only husband of 36 years, who is always there and has spent so many hours at the kitchen table with me, talking and reacting and keeping me on track. "Remember, you're writing about productive meetings—not just humor and laughs."

Special thanks go to the following:

☺ Daniel, Aaron, and Josh Feigelson, my three grown sons, who have provided so much joy and so many humorous examples to share with others in my presentations.

☺ Sara, Hadas, Yonatan, and Leslie, the newest members of the Feigelson family, who continue to expand the sources of loving laughter in our lives.

☺ The countless others in classrooms, workshops, speaking audiences, meetings, and social occasions who have provided the living laboratories to test out the ideas in the book.

☺ And to all of you who at one time or another asked, "How is the book coming?" Don't underestimate the importance of that question: It certainly kept me thinking about my progress—or lack of it. Knowing that you cared made all the difference.

I hope the ideas presented here will make a difference for you.

SHEILA FEIGELSON
Ann Arbor, Michigan
December 1998

Introduction

It's amazing to me that what started out as a personal list of my favorite ways to make meetings and teaching more enjoyable became the book you are holding.

It all began when a teacher friend said, "Sheila, you should write a book with all your ideas and quotes and examples for making meetings more fun. You've got so many of them." She was right.

Meetings have intrigued me for a long time. I think my first formal one took place when I was in 2nd grade at John Hay Elementary School in Minneapolis, Minnesota. We were studying community helpers and held elections for class officers. (Yes, I was president.) That apparently was the beginning of a sustained interest in leadership, group dynamics, and the fields of education and interpersonal communication.

Since that time, of course, I've attended many more meetings and gatherings in various capacities: as a student leader, classroom teacher, university instructor, supervisor, partner in a consulting business, member of professional associations, Cub Scout Den mother, community volunteer, mom of three grown sons, and wife of one caring husband. When I look back on all those situations, it's clear to me that *the most productive—and enjoyable—meetings are those where there is some fun along with getting the work done.*

What This Book Is About

I started writing this book with the notion that it would be something small you could easily browse while having a cup of coffee. I had in mind that busy meeting planners would like a little book with a few ideas for lightening up their meetings. But like most small ideas, this one grew and grew as I considered various questions.

1

☺ What is so important about humor, laughter, and fun?

☺ What kinds of meetings can benefit from a little lightheartedness?

☺ When is levity inappropriate—and when might it actually backfire?

☺ Exactly how can people "lighten up" without becoming too silly? What can facilitators do to invite participants to bring along a smile?

The answers to these and other questions are what this book is about.

Chapter 1 explains the benefits of humor and the importance of planning mindfully for its use in meetings. I also discuss the distinctions between helpful and hurtful humor. Chapter 2 presents four different types of meetings and the various purposes of each. I focus on the idea that you must look carefully at a meeting's primary purpose and a host of related factors when thinking about how to plan for humorous elements.

Chapters 3–12 offer various ways for inviting laughter at appropriate times: before the meeting day, during the meeting itself, and afterwards. Chapter 3 describes ways to elicit a smile before the day of your gathering, which then encourages attendees to show up in a positive frame of mind. Chapter 4 includes many different ideas and tips for injecting humor into the beginning of the meeting before calling the group together. Starting with the arrival of the very first person, this chapter

covers initial greetings, name badges, interactive surveys, and finding a place to sit.

Chapter 5 focuses on ways to introduce the participants. It suggests a number of playful ways to introduce people to each other, including the use of birthdays, vowels, phone numbers, and things to say about themselves besides their names. In Chapter 6 you'll find a variety of materials to help you bring humor into the meeting business itself, including the use of playful props and unexpected inserts in reports and minutes.

In some meetings there are times when you want to create new groupings. Chapter 7 presents unique ways to subdivide a large group into smaller ones. Resist the old count-off-by-threes; learn some new techniques that will ease tension at the same time.

Chapter 8 presents ideas and tips on how to turn the food component into an opportunity for connection and laughter. You can serve "fun" foods, as well as decorate the serving area with fun objects. On a related topic, Chapter 9 suggests some ways to give people the break they need (and deserve) while bringing them back on time and ready to begin refreshed.

Chapter 10 offers suggestions on how to conclude the meeting on a positive note and invite people to leave with a smile. Chapter 11 talks about how thank-you notes and other gestures can help people continue to feel positive about the meeting and look forward to coming back next time. Chapter 12 closes with some reminders of why humor is so important. It offers encouragement to plan for laughter in your next meeting and details two examples where participants had fun while getting the job done. Appendixes A and B and the Resources offer many suggestions for lightening up your meetings.

Remember, though, that if a meeting is poorly run, it's not going to be fun, no matter how many cartoons, trinkets, and clever sayings you use.

Masterful Meeting Managers

In *Making Meetings Work*, Professor John Tropman (1996) describes his fascinating study of what he calls "Master Meeting Managers"—women and men who run great meetings. Tropman was interested to learn about what makes meetings good and how things can be made right: "I observed, talked with, interviewed and participated with meeting experts in the United States and Canada to find out what they did to make their meetings excellent and productive" (p. x). At the same time, he notes, he had plenty of opportunities to observe the work of "non-experts" in the meeting arena.

The "Meeting Masters" were labeled "experts" because they stood out when he asked people for suggestions about whom he should observe. "They stood out because they ran meetings that stood out" (Tropman, 1996, p. x). The Meeting Masters he saw came from government, for-profit groups, and the non-profit sector. They came from all kinds of organizations: universities, big and small companies, religious organizations, and the military.

While the experts felt that their own areas were unique—that is, what worked in a for-profit company might not work in a non-profit organization, or what worked in the military might not work with a governing board—Tropman found that "the experts in different settings were using essentially the same techniques. Underneath the unique features of each organizational type, there was much in common" (1996, p. xi).

The practices used by the experts, he says, are really simple. Anyone can apply them. If you practice them, you will, as one expert said, at least "be able to get as little done as you do now in half the time!"

Tropman's research showed that the excellent meetings almost always contained four features (1996, p. x):

1. Their meetings were characterized by accomplishment. Decisions got made in these groups.

2. There was little decision rework. The group did not have to get together to decide again something that had already been decided or, as likely, had been avoided.

3. The decisions were *good.* There was a feeling, buttressed by reality as time passed, that the work of the group was of high quality. These were not just decisions made to "get something done." They were

thoughtful and reasoned, and they were actions that made a difference to the bureau, company, or agency.

4. *People had fun! These were meetings that members looked forward to. There was a sense of enjoyment and involvement. Members felt that their time was well spent.* [italics mine]

☺   ☺   ☺

Energize Your Meetings with Laughter focuses primarily on the last point: How to have fun. What can we do to purposely create a positive climate, a sense of enjoyment and involvement? How can we invite a little more productive laughter to our meetings? To find the answers, I invite you to read on.

1

Making Room for Laughter

Mr. Anders knew that Wednesday's staff meeting was going to be rough. The recent teacher's strike had been nasty. Along with other principals in the district, he was facing tough decisions about budget, program, and personnel cuts. And on top of all that, the weather was lousy! Something *had* to be done to break the tension.

As he was gathering some last-minute items for the meeting, Mr. Anders noticed the large paper cutter in the corner of his office. Hesitating for just a moment, he walked over to it, took a deep breath, leaned down, and whacked off the bottom half of his necktie.

After slipping on his sport coat and walking into the meeting room, he called the group to order and stared ahead with a deadpan look. Then, with a twinkle in his eye, he shook his head, opened his coat a little, and pointed to his tie.

"These program cuts are having unexpected effects on all of us!" he said. Then he smiled and shrugged his shoulders in a familiar "now what?" manner. Of course, staff members laughed at this preplanned bit of humor, and the ice was broken. More important, the message came through: We're all going to get through this together. "Life will go on, and so will we," Mr. Anders emphasized.

What a smart leader! Mr. Anders knew his group, and he knew that levity would be extremely important for any constructive business to take place that day. By gently poking fun at himself, he helped others lighten up and relax enough so that they could get on with their serious business.

Your Meeting History

You've probably been to meetings where someone did or said just the right thing at just the right time to ease the tension. Maybe *you* were the one who did this! But how many times have you endured tense, dull, or going-nowhere meetings? How often have you attended meetings that just seemed to drag, where nothing much happened? People listened, looked attentive, and even took notes. Yet on the balance, nothing was accomplished. Nothing was learned. Little got done, and it wasn't much fun. You could have just stayed home or back in your office or classroom and it wouldn't have mattered.

Take a moment to think about one of the worst meetings you ever attended. Choose just one, for now. Which of the following items explains why you rated it so low?

- It didn't start on time.
- The purpose wasn't clear.
- We didn't stick to the agenda.
- There was no agenda.
- The participants weren't introduced.
- People didn't seem to pay attention to each other.
- There were too many people.
- There were too few people.
- The right people weren't there.
- The speakers rambled.
- People were rude to each other.
- The temperature in the room was uncomfortable.
- The location was inconvenient.
- The chairs were uncomfortable.
- It was difficult to hear and to see what was going on.
- The refreshments were unhealthy.
- The refreshments were skimpy.
- *What* refreshments?
- Someone was on a "power" or "ego" trip.
- It was too long, too formal, too stuffy, too intimidating.
- People didn't do their homework.
- Reports were boring. We could have read them ourselves.
- There wasn't any fun!
- We didn't get the work done.

How are you feeling as you go through this list? A little down? These kinds of memories can be depressing! Fortunately, we know that not all meetings are that bad. Many of them are highly productive. Think about one of the best meetings you ever attended, or a good meeting you attend with some regularity. Which items explain why you rate it so highly?

- ☺ The purpose is clearly stated.
- ☺ Advanced planning is evident.
- ☺ People respect each other.
- ☺ People listen.
- ☺ They arrive on time.
- ☺ They do their homework.
- ☺ Enough time is allotted for business.
- ☺ People stick with the task at hand.
- ☺ The leader knows how to involve the participants.
- ☺ The reports are brief, interesting, and to the point.
- ☺ There are good, healthy, ample refreshments.

☺ The meeting place is comfortable.

☺ There is often a surprise—a safe, pleasant kind of surprise.

☺ There is appropriate lightness, good humor, laughter, and fun.

☺ Most important, the work gets done.

How are you feeling now? More optimistic?

Consider this: What happens when there is no levity or shared laughter at a meeting? What happens when everything is carried out with a grim sense of purpose? Many of us feel that when there is no element of enjoyment in a meeting, participants become bored. And they become cranky. They don't think creatively; minds wander; no one offers any suggestions. Time drags, and ultimately, people just tune out. If you attended this gathering voluntarily, the dull, no-fun meeting is guaranteed to discourage you from returning.

Now consider what happens when people share some laughs and genuinely enjoy a meeting. Like others who have answered this question, you may have noticed that people are more creative when there is some fun and good-natured humor in the program. Time goes by quickly. People participate. They become energized, and tension dissipates. Communication improves. Most people look forward to working on the tasks, and they have a renewed sense of being in control of something. Most important, they will eagerly come to the meeting again. *Simply stated, people are more likely to show up when they can look forward to having a little fun at their meetings and gatherings.*

Easy Elements of Fun

One of the easiest ways to make sure there's an element of fun is to provide some type of lighthearted item for participants. It can be as simple as a cartoon at each person's place or one that's displayed on a screen. It can be an edible treat such as a happy-face cookie. Or you can read a short humorous piece and have copies available for each person afterwards.

One supervisor begins his staff meetings with a funny thought for the day. Another shares the responsibility with the group: Each member takes a turn bringing in the "joke-of-the-meeting." People actually look forward to planning for their turn to be the "jester." In one department of a large school district, staff members keep their spirits up by acknowledging their need to increase the "f-factor" (translated as: "Let's have some fun around here today!").

With a little fun, meeting participants are more likely to be creative and productive. Appropriately timed and used, humor enlivens and energizes. It reduces tension and turns negatives into positives. Humor helps us communicate and cope with stress. Shared laughter enables people to connect in positive ways.

Of course, these benefits result when humor is used appropriately—when it's good-natured and inclusive. Positive humor builds trust, which is critical for encouraging participation in meetings. We are more likely to speak up and to offer our help when we trust that others will accept us.

Destructive and Constructive Humor

Are you skeptical? Think about it: Why would you ever *not* want to encourage laughter at your meeting? Or why would you ever want to discourage participants from laughing? Some people say:

- There's no time! We have to get our work done.
- Someone might be offended.
- It's not our style. We just don't usually do it.
- None of us knows how to make people lighten up.
- We don't want to look foolish.
- The nature of our work is very sensitive and serious.
- It's not necessary.
- It may cost us more money than we expected.

Certainly there are times when lightheartedness is inappropriate. When the topic at hand is bad news, with serious life-threatening, life-changing consequences, it is not the time to try to be humorous. When health and security are at risk, your attempt to be funny will most likely be viewed as condescending

and destructive. And for sure, when your attempts at humor interfere with getting the job done (no matter what kind of job), they will be most unwelcome. As with most matters in life, timing is everything.

In addition, we need to be careful to distinguish between hurtful and helpful humor. Joel Goodman, founder and director of the Humor Project in Saratoga Springs, New York, and editor of the quarterly publication *Laughing Matters*, notes that there is a marked difference between humor that is constructive and humor that is destructive (Goodman, 1981, p. 12). It's the difference between laughing *with* others and laughing *at* others. Goodman offers a very useful checklist to help understand the differences (Figure 1.1).

I created "The GIVE Principle" to highlight the differences.

Constructive humor:

invites a **G**ood laugh;
     Includes everyone;
       is **V**ictimless,
   and is **E**nergizing.

A good laugh leaves you feeling good about yourself. It is both a physical and emotional pleasure. It lifts your spirits. It's funny and enjoyable.

A bad laugh physiologically releases the same enzymes and works the muscles, but it leaves you feeling strangely empty. It does not make you feel better about yourself. You might be laughing really hard with someone,

Figure 1.1
── *Hurtful vs. Helpful Humor* ──

Laughing *at* others:	Laughing *with* others:
1. going for the jugular vein	1. going for the jocular vein
2. based on contempt and insensitivity	2. based on caring and empathy
3. destroys confidence through put-downs	3. builds confidence
4. excludes some people	4. involves people in the fun
5. a person does not have a choice in being made the butt of a joke	5. a person makes a choice to be the butt of a joke (as in "laughing at yourself")
6. abusing—offends people	6. amusing—invites people to laugh
7. sarcastic	7. supportive
8. divides people	8. brings people closer
9. leads to one-downsmanship cycle	9. leads to positive repartee
10. reinforces stereotypes by singling out a particular group as the "butt"	10. pokes fun at universal human foibles

Source: Adapted with permission from *Laughing Matters*, by J. Goodman, 1981. Saratoga Springs, NY: The Humor Project.

but typically you're laughing derisively *at* someone else. You're laughing at the expense of another, even if that person is not present.

When you walk into a meeting room and a group in the corner is laughing, your first impulse may be to feel left out and uncomfortable. It's likely, however, that people are not purposely trying to exclude you; it's merely the timing of your arrival that unintentionally prompts that response. A considerate person would sense this and immediately let you in on the joke: "Come, join us! Pat here was just telling the funniest story."

True exclusionary humor is intentional and occurs when just a few "in" people know the reference. It's the knowing wink, the nod, the roll of the eyes, or other nonverbal messages that pass only among a few. To the outsider, this can be rude and hurtful. Inclusive humor makes sure *everyone* is in on the joke or source of amusement. Exclusive laughter leaves people out.

Constructive humor has no victim. It's the kind of humor where we're affectionately laughing *at* and *with* ourselves and not at someone else's expense. We're laughing at the human condition, not at the condition of a human. And we're inviting others to laugh with us. It's truly shared humor and laughter, like the phone call I got from my good friend, Geri. "You're not going to believe this!" she exclaimed. "I followed your chicken soup recipe exactly. I used a whole chicken, cut-up carrots, onions, celery, dill, salt, pepper, garlic, and even a little ketchup, and I let it simmer for about three hours. The house smelled delicious, and I could hardly wait to serve it. As soon as it cooled, I put the colander in the sink and started to strain it. I poured the entire pot . . . aaarghhh!"

"You poured it right down the kitchen sink!" I finished.

The soup was gone, but the shared experience is one we both savored.

"Good" laughter is energizing and invigorating. When we laugh heartily, we bring oxygen into our bodies and work our muscles. In *Anatomy of an Illness*, Norman Cousins (1979) described it as "internal jogging."

Hearty laughter is good for us. Most often, we feel energized and more eager to get on with our task. Constructive, helpful humor is like a drink of water when we're thirsty or the cup of coffee that gets us going in the morning. We can still feel it as we go about our business. Destructive humor—which hurts rather than helps—is draining and leaves us feeling flat and empty. It is de-energizing.

Give Humor a Chance

For humor to be most effective at a meeting, it has to yield a smile and, hopefully, a good laugh that includes everybody. It's victimless, and it creates energy to continue with the business at hand. When planning for laughter at your meeting, keep this in mind. "GIVE" the opportunity for humor to work and not to destroy.

Remember, too, that effective humor never dominates the agenda. It knows its place and never overstays its welcome. Respectful of people's time and the task at hand, good meeting leaders do not let laughter get in the way of serious business. They skillfully use humor to keep the meeting on track and the group attentive and involved. And if you're concerned that you don't have a sense of humor that can pull all this off, keep in mind Goodman's observation: "I see humor as a set of skills, attitudes and guidelines that we can consciously access, and like any set of skills, humor can be nurtured through practice" (1983, p. 12).

Give Stress the Door

The skillful use of humor is an important part of working through difficult times. A few years ago, I helped a stressed-out staff in Michigan learn to use humor to reduce stress in their workplace. At that time, Michigan's budget for human services was drastically cut. People in all the human services were feeling the effects, especially the director of a state-funded agency that provided important health services to teenage mothers. She realized that her staff was terribly demoralized. They were hard-working and dedicated, and they were very concerned about the future of the program.

The director called to ask if I could do a short presentation at her next staff meeting on ways to lighten up in stressful times. I wasn't sure that I could be of help; the situation seemed so bleak. But I accepted the task and prepared for something fun that would give the staff a much needed "laugh break" and at the same time generate some ideas for things they could do on their own to keep up morale.

On the appointed day, I arrived in time for the beginning of the staff meeting and updates from each of the 16 people there. Each "progress report" was more depressing than the last! The grim news went on for an hour, and there was not one smile in the room, not even from me.

At last it was my turn. I acknowledged how awful things were and suggested two alternatives: We can declare the situation hopeless and quit, or we can go on and try to find the good parts. This produced some reluctant smiles. I pointed out how shared laughter can help us get a necessary break and perhaps provide a new perspective.

I then asked them to talk about what laughter does for us. They came up with quite a list. Laughter relaxes us, makes us feel better, helps us think more clearly, builds camaraderie, and makes the day go faster. This led to a discussion of the ways that we can purposely encourage smiles and good feelings. One of those ways is by talking about topics that evoke pleasant and fun memories. So, it was natural to pursue that topic with this staff. In groups of three, they discussed and recollected various toys, games, and amusements from their own childhood. They shared memories of spinning tops, building snow forts, and playing hide-and-go-seek.

Within five minutes, the mood changed from gloom to gladness, relaxation, and even a note of hopefulness. Sometimes, just remembering that we can laugh in times of tremendous stress helps us feel more optimistic and certainly more positive. It was amazing how quickly clouds lifted once people started to talk about fun topics. And I was impressed to hear all the ideas they later identified to make their work place and meetings more uplifting. One of the simplest, most powerful suggestions was to begin each meeting by having each person describe something positive that they had experienced since the last meeting. Someone else suggested bringing flowers for the reception desk. Another suggestion was to simply remember to smile and say "good morning" to each other.

☺   ☺   ☺

What's the point of all this? That there are things we can purposely do to create a more positive, hopeful meeting climate. We can consciously invite laughter in order to warm people up to the tasks, help them feel comfortable together, and be more productive.

Most people would agree that when there is an element of fun along with a sense of accomplishment, meetings are more enjoyable. We look forward to getting together again. As the title character observes in the classic children's movie, *Willy Wonka and the Chocolate Factory*, "A little nonsense now and then is relished by the wisest men."

How do people have fun in a meeting? By employing their own sense of humor and playfulness—appropriately. Is it risky to put some fun on the agenda? Certainly, but there is a difference between humor that moves us toward goals and humor that blocks us. It seems even more risky not to plan for humor. And it seems especially risky to keep the proceedings dull, dry, and boring! You can—and should—plan for the presence of wholesome, good-hearted laughter, humor, and fun. The rest of this book will help you do that.

2

Four Major Types of Meetings

Human beings are social creatures. Not only do we like to be with people, we *need* to be with people. It's part of our basic nature.

You can be sure that as you're reading this, a group is meeting somewhere. Maybe they're writing a strategic plan. Perhaps they've come together to learn new skills or to get acquainted with one another. Whether your next meeting is a gathering to make decisions, network, learn new information, or celebrate a success, you may gain from this chapter ways to optimize the benefits of humor, laughter, and a little playfulness.

Why Do People Meet?

The United States was built on meetings; a democracy cannot run without them. We rely on ourselves and on our designated representatives to make collective decisions in many arenas of our lives. Our traditions support group gatherings to raise issues, explore pros and cons, consider alternatives, and choose a course of action. This happens in business, education, volunteer organizations, government, and even families.

People get together for any number of reasons: to visit, play cards, go to a ball game, have a party, sing, eat, pray, mourn, or watch a parade. Usually, we don't consider these kinds of activities to be "meetings." We're more likely to think of them as social gatherings or get-togethers. But a gathering can become a "meeting" when it has a stated purpose and a desired outcome, such as making decisions, sharing information, expanding professional and social networks, or celebrating achievements or events. Though gatherings can be planned or spontaneous, meetings are most definitely planned—at least, they should be!

Usually the word "meeting" suggests a group of people, even as few as two or three persons. The size of the group, whether it's 5 or 500, influences the choice of location for the meeting. Think of all the places where meetings are held: in board rooms, classrooms, libraries, community centers, auditoriums, hotels, conference centers, restaurants, living rooms, and around the kitchen table. More and more meetings are taking place via telephone and the Internet. As teleconferencing grows, we won't have to be in the same place to meet. Even today, technology allows us to have meetings while traveling in cars or waiting at airports.

Who Meets?

Which of these groups is most familiar to you? Meetings of:

- staff
- teams
- committees
- school boards
- teachers
- trainers
- directors
- managers
- business associates
- professional colleagues
- students
- campers
- parents
- neighborhood residents
- families
- partners
- bosses
- supervisors
- employees
- administrators
- leaders
- salespeople
- helpers
- technicians

Obviously, we have many opportunities for getting together with others—for better or worse!

Four Meeting Elements

Regardless of who meets, most of us recognize that meetings include at least three elements: the participants, the tasks to accomplish, and the physical environment in which the meeting occurs. Meeting planners also need to attend to a fourth element that often is overlooked: the tone of the meeting.

Most planners concentrate on the participants, the tasks to be accomplished, and the physical environment, leaving a positive emotional environment to chance. They hope for the best without necessarily doing much to ensure an affirmative, supportive climate. Yet this is a critical aspect of the meeting environment (see Figure 2.1).

For each of these elements, we rely on special skills. The tasks of problem solving and decision making require analytical and organizational skills. Building on the diverse strengths and talents of the various individuals in any meeting requires comprehensive interpersonal and team-building skills. And arranging the environment for maximum participation requires skills of organizing space and time.

Likewise, creating an emotional tone that frees people to be focused, creative, and productive requires skills of timing, listening, humor, and playfulness. It calls for being serious but not solemn. As Joel Goodman reminds us, "Seven days without laughter makes one weak" (1995, p. 2). Balancing a sense of serious purpose and a sense of humor is a challenge; and this book will help you find ways

Figure 2.1
Four Elements of Meetings

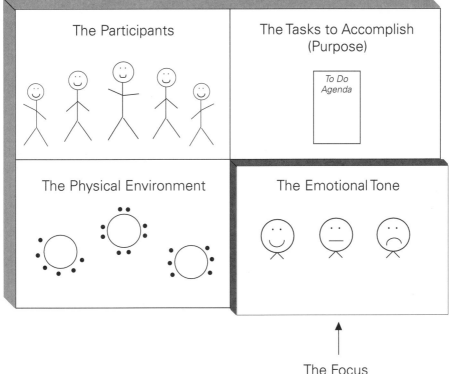

The Participants

The Tasks to Accomplish
(Purpose)

To Do
Agenda

The Physical Environment

The Emotional Tone

The Focus
of This Book

to do that. Even meetings involving disputes or serious negotiations can benefit from a positive meeting climate and occasional relief from sober proceedings.

Humor and Four Major Types of Meetings

Regardless of the group, size, or location, meetings are usually held for a primary reason. When planning for humor and fun, I find it useful to distinguish four major types of meetings, based on their main purpose. They are:

☺ *Decision-making meetings, where the main purpose is to solve problems, make decisions, and plan.* Boards, councils, faculties, task forces, committees, teams, associates, partners, and staff often conduct this sort of meeting.

☺ *Networking meetings, where the main purpose is to meet other people and build relationships.* Types of groups that hold this kind of meeting include professional associations, civic groups, chambers of commerce, and support groups.

☺ *Learning meetings, where the main purpose is to gain information, knowledge, and skills.* Students, adult learners, trainees, employees, and teams often are involved in this type of meeting.

☺ *Celebration meetings, where the main purpose is to honor someone, recognize accomplishments, and enjoy the time together.* Types of groups that meet to celebrate include colleagues, friends, family, and associates who are attending awards ceremonies, reunions, baby and bridal showers, weddings, birthday parties, commencements, receptions, or retirements.

Certainly, a single meeting may share many elements of all four types, but each meeting type differs from one another in focus and goals. Carefully attending to the differences in the function of each meeting helps determine how humor can be an appropriate part of the agenda.

Decision-Making Meetings

The primary business of decision-making meetings is to reach conclusions, solve problems, define strategies, or make plans. Decision-making meetings range from a committee setting the date for its annual fundraiser to the U.S. Congress passing legislation affecting the entire population. Decisions can be as simple as determining a menu for a spe-

cial event or as complex as detailing logistics for the Olympics. Many tasks are required on the decision-making agenda: gathering and sharing information, planning, testing out ideas, and reviewing.

Boards, councils, faculties, task forces, teams, and committees all focus on making decisions. In the process they explore ideas, gather and review information, solve problems, and make plans. Their main mission, however, is to make decisions.

No matter how well participants do or don't know each other, there is always some tension when people get together in meetings. In a decision-making meeting, the primary sources of tension include concerns like "Is this the right course of action?" "How much time will this take?" and "How will it affect me?" The very nature of a decision can be a source of stress, especially if it is complex or controversial. The competencies of the participants and, of course, their relationships with one another also affect their degree of comfort or discomfort.

People arrive at their meetings in all kinds of moods, ranging from eager to be there to eager to be out of there! Participants in decision meetings are usually time conscious. Whatever they see as not contributing to the stated purpose may be viewed as extraneous and, consequently, annoying.

Still, we often assume that when people come to these meetings they're ready to work. Not necessarily! We may need to warm them to the tasks. We need to create a climate that encourages active listening, creative thinking, and sound decisions.

In addition to having a clear agenda with timelines, relevant information, and processes that move things along, a decision-making meeting benefits from appropriate playfulness. It goes a long way toward creating a relaxed mood that allows people to focus on the serious work at hand. Well-placed humor and shared laughter can reduce the tension and help participants keep their perspective. Sharing a laugh does wonders for people.

One supervisor I know of was well aware of this. At a meeting she had called to talk about morale problems and lack of teamwork, she brought a pair of work gloves. The only problem was that the fingers had been sewn together. When someone asked why, she explained that when a person put them on, there would be no way of "pointing a finger" at someone else.

A training director with a sense of fun knew that his group would need something more than charts, graphs, and lists to keep them alert as they planned their annual budget requests. To relieve the monotony of looking at all the figures, he prepared a transparency of a weather map. When the timing was right, he placed it on the projector and acted surprised when it showed on the screen. Then, he pretended that he was a television weather announcer and gave a quick, animated forecast. It caught his audience off guard, and they had a great laugh together. They appreciated his wit and sensitivity to enlivening their meeting. And they got back to work with renewed energy.

Networking Meetings

The primary goal of a networking meeting is to enable people with similar interests to meet one another. Cynthia D'Amour, author of the book *Networking* (1997), describes the process as "a human thing. It's about building relationships that are mutually beneficial" (p. 1). The overriding tone of such a meeting is "How can we be helpful to each other?" and "How can we get the help we need?" Professional associations, service organizations, sororities, fraternities, civic groups, business associations, hobby clubs, chambers of commerce, religious groups, self-help groups, and support groups all have networking as a major purpose.

People attend networking meetings to meet each other and have meaningful conversations. That is, they talk about things beyond the weather and ball game scores. They actively seek ways to develop new relationships and learn how they might be helpful to each other. Conversations revolve around common interests and activities, the kinds of help they need, or the kinds of help they can offer.

Tension in networking meetings usually stems from greeting new people and finding useful things to talk about. Even the most extroverted participants can find it a challenge to decide what to say and to whom. And shy participants would definitely welcome help to open up conversation.

Humor in networking meetings can ease the tension that comes from meeting new people, finding a place to sit, and knowing what to say. Make it easy to start a conversation. For example, room arrangements can support or sabotage successful networking meetings. Round tables encourage conversation better than oblong ones. Food, decorations, and displays give people something to talk about. And you don't have to leave conversation to chance, either. Appendix A contains some helpful conversation starters for meetings such as this.

You might consider providing name tags with humorous sayings or funny stickers. Encourage people to ask each other about them. For example, ask people to write their name and something else on the tag, such as a significant number, a favorite place where they have lived, or even a favorite childhood amusement. (Chapters 4 and 5 detail many fun ways to lighten the initial greeting process, especially for networking.)

In your role as a leader, you can introduce people to each other by mentioning something they might have in common: "Jane, I want you to meet Joe. You share something in common: You were both at the national conference last winter where we heard that great speaker who talked about humor. Remember that?" This of course provides an opportunity for the pair to begin a comfortable conversation about a safe, pleasant topic.

As a participant in a networking meeting, you can wear or bring something with you to catch attention and invite a chuckle. Any humorous object will work: an unusual pin, a funny necktie, or a hat. You also might consider a funny business card, trinket, or gadget that you can show to others.

Learning Meetings

The primary business of learning meetings is to raise awareness, share information, and learn or develop a skill or strategy. The leader's goal is to help participants learn, understand, or perform, and he or she is responsible for creating a safe environment for learning. This can be done in many ways. One important approach is to articulate some of the fears that learners might have and the questions that will be addressed. Students in schools, colleges, and adult education programs; convention delegates; participants in workshops, seminars, and conferences; and employees in training all engage in learning.

Learners worry about things such as how they will be evaluated: "If I don't know this, am I stupid?" "Will I be able to understand this?" "How am I doing?" "Will I pass the course?" For leaders, concerns center around how they will present material, hold participants' attention, and then know that what they've offered has actually been understood.

Well-timed and well-placed humor creates the kind of climate that invites participation by putting people at ease. In one of the best books on this subject, *The Laughing Classroom*, Loomans and Kolberg (1993) remind us that humor, laughter, and a little playfulness have tremendous benefits for learners. Among them are that shared laughter and play will "maintain a high attention level, relieve physical and mental stress, build rapport, increase retention, bring new insights, allow for pleasurable learning, and increase a feeling of hope" (p. 33).

Novelty brings laughter to otherwise repetitive, dull situations. In learning situations, novelty can be used for both presenting and reviewing information. For example, one teacher I know pretends she's a game-show host while reviewing information. When a student comes up with a wrong answer, she kiddingly says, "I'm sorry. You've just lost the $4,000 prize, but we do have another prize for you!"

To get the attention of his students, one trainer likes to use a pen as a pretend microphone. He acts as though he is testing it, and he talks very softly, saying, "Can you hear me in the back of the room?" It does the job: Students tune in with a smile, and they're ready to hear what he's going to say.

Another teacher I know always includes a humorous question or quotation somewhere in the middle of the exam, unrelated to the topic. When he hears chuckles, he knows how far the students are in the test. And the students appreciate the lighthearted break in the otherwise serious activity.

Celebration Meetings

The primary business of celebration meetings is to recognize achievement, commemorate special events, and bestow honors and awards. Such meetings take many forms, and anyone and everyone attends these kinds of meetings.

Groups of colleagues, friends, relatives, and strangers attend awards ceremonies, retirement dinners, bridal and baby showers, birthday parties, reunions, and inductions.

A celebration meeting implies some type of planned program for everyone in attendance, some form of shared happy experience for all. But have you ever been to a celebration and felt that it could have been for just about anyone or anything, like a generic wedding shower or awards ceremony? You can make your celebration meeting special both for the honorees and the other participants by doing something that is unique and memorable.

More than in other types of meetings, celebrations have fun as the focal point. People arrive expecting to have a good time. Still, even celebratory gatherings can have some tension. The honorees may be nervous about receiving attention. Some of those attending may not know anyone except the guest of honor. And there's often unacknowledged tension when participants feel that they should be enjoying themselves, but they're not! Meeting planners need to help everyone have a good time.

We often think that at a celebration, everyone knows each other. But it's not always true. In fact, I've been to celebrations where I knew only a few people, and I wished that someone had done something to introduce all of us. Humor is naturally useful for enhancing the festive mood and for helping people feel comfortable and welcomed. A well-placed, light touch helps people enjoy themselves.

For example, at an awards ceremony, one group always includes some made-up humorous awards for unsung heroes: "This special award goes to Mr. X for continually managing the thermostat at our meetings."

At one gathering in honor of a new bride and groom, name tags were color coded so that guests could immediately identify how people were related: friends and relatives of the bride or the groom. During the dinner, each person was introduced and was given an opportunity to say how they were related, name places they had lived, and tell a little anecdote about the honorees. This provided a fun touch and allowed each person to make yet another connection.

Figure 2.2 (see next page) is a matrix that summarizes the four major meeting types and some of the factors that influence your decisions on when and how to use humor.

Multiple Purposes

While each type of meeting has a predominant purpose, most have multiple purposes. For example, a decision-making meeting focuses primarily on making decisions. In order to make informed decisions, however, information must be shared. Thus, there also is a learning component. People have to know something about each other to build trust. And certainly there ought to be some form of celebration or acknowledgment of the work accomplished, be it large or small. Sometimes a simple "thumbs up" is sufficient. The best meetings also include all *these*

elements: action, camaraderie, learning, and laughter.

Unfortunately, many people get so focused on the *main* purpose of a meeting that they neglect supporting ones. Or they get so distracted by the *supporting* purposes that they don't accomplish the meeting's primary goals. With so many demands on our time these days, we are more conscious than ever of the importance of well-run meetings and gatherings. We feel cheated and insulted when meetings waste our time and when they don't accomplish what they are supposed to.

The Boy Scouts and Girl Scouts are good examples of meetings that accomplish multiple purposes. As you look at the structure of their troop meetings, it's no surprise why both organizations have been around for a long time. Their meetings include all four of the basic meeting purposes:

- *Decision-making*: planning for upcoming events, setting dues, assigning responsibilities for the next meeting;
- *Networking*: having a chance to talk and play together in an organized fashion;
- *Learning*: developing new skills such as knot-tying; and
- *Celebration*: awards ceremonies for presenting badges and achieving new ranks.

While each part does not take up the same amount of time, each contributes to the success of the meeting.

Figure 2.3 (see p. 22) summarizes some things that are common to all four types of meetings.

Figure 2.2
Four Types of Meetings and the Role of Humor

	Decision-Making	Networking	Learning	Celebrating
What is the primary purpose of the meeting?	• To solve problems • To make decisions • To plan and review	• To meet other people • To build relationships	• To raise awareness • To share information • To learn new information • To increase skills	• To recognize accomplishments • To honor someone • To enjoy the event and each other's company
What kinds of groups meet?	• Teams • Staffs • Task forces • Boards and councils • Committees	• Professional associations • Business and civic groups • Support groups • Social clubs	• Students • Adult learners • Trainees • Employees • Team members	• Work groups • Colleagues • Friends • Neighbors • Families
What are primary sources of tension at meetings?	• Having to make a decision • Needing to accomplish a task • Not trusting others • Being unclear of the task • Not knowing the consequences • Not having criteria for success	• Meeting new people • Fearing the unknown • Feeling shy • Not having credentials • Lacking credibility • Lacking experience	• Worrying • Feeling bored • Being annoyed by the teaching style • Feeling uncertain	• Ensuring that each person enjoys himself or herself • Helping everyone share in the joy • Not feeling comfortable in the group • Not knowing what to expect
What is the primary role of humor and laughter?	• To reduce tension • To enliven the meeting • To promote creative thinking • To re-energize • To unify	• To create a pleasant atmosphere • To put people at ease • To create connections • To build cohesiveness	• To reduce stress • To gain and maintain attention • To communicate more easily • To improve memory • To refresh or provide a break	• To relax • To allow people to help each other have a good time • To enhance good feelings • To entertain • To increase the joy of being together

Figure 2.3
——————— *What Is Common to All Four Types of Meetings?* ———————

Sources of tension for participants:	What's not getting done back at the office, or home, or in the classroom? What do I have to do when I return? What's waiting for me? What I am missing by being here?
Implication for participants:	The meeting had better be worth my time!
Implication for leader:	This meeting has to be organized and well-run. It needs to have an element of fun!
When to have fun and still be productive:	As people arrive As participants are introduced During a break When dividing into smaller groups When serving food During brainstorming, summaries, and conclusions As people leave When giving a report
How to lighten up and make the meeting appropriately fun:	By using props, printed materials, visual displays, audio By serving fun foods By reading or telling something humorous By talking about fun topics By doing something novel, a safe surprise

Faulty Assumptions

We often get so caught up in a single objective that we overlook the other meeting purposes. Here are some false assumptions we frequently make:

• When people come to our meetings, they're ready to make decisions.

• If people have been to previous meetings, they already know each other.

• If people look like they're paying attention, they actually are.

• If people are attending our celebrations, they are enjoying themselves.

As a meeting planner, you can sit back and hope your participants will be attentive, involved, and productive. Or you can employ specific techniques to increase the chances of success. You can do some things to make sure that people know one another so they can relax enough to risk participation. You can use a lighthearted approach to create an inviting climate where people enjoy themselves and tune in to the work of the meeting.

When can you create this inviting climate? Opportunities abound before, during, and after your event. You can purposely plan for laughter. And that is the precisely what the rest of this book is about: ways you can plan for a little fun in order to get the job done.

Seven Planning Questions

We can wait and hope for something funny to happen in meetings, and we can be prepared to seize this opportunity for fun. Or we can actually *plan* for something fun to happen. As you know by now, this book is about purposely planning for fun in meetings. I have found there are at least seven questions to ask when determining the kind of "humor injection" you want to plan.

1. What is the main purpose of the meeting? It may be one or more of the four primary meeting types: to make decisions, network, learn new information or skills, or celebrate an accomplishment.

2. Why are the people there, and what is their relationship to each other? Their attendance may be voluntary, or it may be required. They may know each other well, somewhat, or not at all. They may be colleagues, bosses, subordinates, friends, or relatives.

3. What is the physical environment like? Is the furniture movable, and are there tables and chairs? Are tables round or oblong?

4. How much time do you have for the meeting, from start to finish?

5. How much preplanning will be required for the "humor injection"? Will you have the time, energy, and inclination to do it?

6. What, really, is the desired outcome of the meeting? By the end, what do you want to have accomplished? How do you want people to feel when they leave? If the group will be meeting again, what will they have to do between this meeting and the next one, if anything?

7. How comfortable are you with planning for something fun? If you are not comfortable doing it, can you delegate the planning to someone else? Do you have ideas for what you might like to do? Do you really want to do anything at all?

Let me invite you into my mind as I plan for lightening up a meeting. Some preliminary questions I ask myself are in plain type; my answers are in parentheses and italics.

• Why are you meeting? (*To begin planning a day-long conference.*)

• What is the primary purpose? Make decisions? Plan? Generate ideas? Review? Meet new people? Get together? Network? Learn? Teach? Train? Share information? Honor? Celebrate? Award? (*To generate ideas.*)

• How will you keep the meeting moving in a productive direction? (*I will plan and print an agenda, listing tasks that have to be done sometime before the event occurs. I'll ask the others what needs to be added. Maybe I'll decorate the agenda with some cartoon characters or happy faces or maybe a clever quote from someone.)*

• How will you create a safe, positive, motivating climate? *(Sit around a table, have some food, remind us that the primary purpose of this meeting is to generate ideas and be able to think about them before we make any decisions at our next meeting.)*

• What will you do to invite laughter, to have a little fun while you get the job done? What kind of "humor injection" will you use? *(I will bring some lollipops and some "Happy Rocks" for each person. I'll also raise the question: What can we do to make sure we have a little fun while getting the job done at our meetings?)*

☺   ☺   ☺

As you can see, it doesn't take much effort to inject a little lightheartedness into the proceedings. The rest of this book explores opportunities for how you can use a humorous, playful approach to create a more trusting, motivating, inviting, effective, and safe meeting climate. When you invite laughter to your meeting, you set the stage for productivity and create the kind of climate that helps to accomplish your meeting goals.

3

Announcing Your Meeting with Flair

Consider the fact that most meetings follow a similar pattern: People arrive, they take care of business, and they leave. Before all of that, they receive notice that the meeting will occur. And following the meeting, they may or may not receive a report of the proceedings, such as minutes or a summary. Sometimes, participants even receive thank-you notes for their contributions to the meeting's success!

All these meeting components—announcement, arrival, the manner of handling business, departure, and follow-up—offer perfect opportunities to introduce a little lightheartedness. Of course, not *all* parts of a meeting have to be full of laughter; that would be too distracting. But if there's no levity at all, your meeting is going to be mighty dull and probably less productive.

The following chapters suggest ways to invite laughter and a lighthearted spirit into your meetings. This chapter focuses on how people receive information about a meeting. The announcement of the meeting itself also can be an invitation to bring along a smile. Whether the announcement is a memo, letter, e-mail, or printed invitation, it influences how the recipient responds. The call to a meeting is a prime opportunity for the meeting leader to create positive anticipation: "Yes! I want to be there!"

Truly Inviting Announcements

Karen Schulte and Carol Bailiff, of the professional development office in the Ann Arbor Public Schools, know the value of making meeting announcements (and meetings) special. Figure 3.1 shows the "non-meeting" invitation they sent to school administrators—with a positive result. Many partici-

Figure 3.1
Announcing a "Non-Meeting"

To: Ann Arbor Building and Central Office Administrators

Anyone out there **TIRED** of meetings?
Are you **TIRED** of running meetings?
Are you **TIRED** of attending meetings?
Anyone out there just plain **TIRED**?

Let's Re-energize!

(Page 1 of folded flyer)

pants came early and stayed late. And I, as the workshop leader, loved every minute of it. (You can read a more detailed description of the workshop in Chapter 12.)

You don't have to be a designer to add a light note to your meeting announcements. A bit of clip art or a humorous quotation can do the trick. Just look through books of quotes, greeting cards, magazines, and the Internet to find pictures and sayings that tickle you. The Resources section of this book contains some of my favorite sources for humor-ous quotations. I especially recommend the works by Robert Byrne (1988), Joel Goodman (1995), Allen Klein (1991), and Steve Wilson (1990). Following are some examples of lively quotations from those and other sources, the kinds of quotations you might consider using on your meeting announcements.

☺ "We don't laugh because we're happy; we're happy because we laugh." —*William James*

☺ "A smile is the shortest distance between two people." —*Victor Borge*

Figure 3.1—continued

Karen S. of Professional Growth and Development would like to invite you . . .

. . . to attend a dinner NON-MEETING on Tuesday, March 12, at Balas 2. We'll relax over dinner from 5:30 to 6:00, and then Sheila Feigelson will engage us in a conversation from 6:00 to 7:30 around techniques to energize our meetings. You'll learn useful ideas concerning:

- The **agenda** and other printed matter
- **Food**
- **Introductions**
- **Breaks**
- **Endings**
- **Humor** and other ways to improve our "over-meetinged" lives

Please e-mail Carol B. by Friday, March 1, if you will be able to join us for this relaxing, enjoyable, and productive **NON-MEETING**.

(Page 2 of flyer)

Note: Adapted by permission of Carol Bailiff and Karen Schulte.

☺ "Things turn out the best for people who make the best of the way things turn out." —*Art Linkletter*

☺ "Sometimes I think I'm indecisive, but I'm not so sure. . . ." —*Unknown*

☺ "The secret to happiness lies not so much in doing what you like, but in liking what you do!" —*Unknown*

☺ "Every day, make one person smile who wasn't expecting to. Maybe that person will be you!" —C. *Leslie Charles*

☺ "Life does not cease to be funny when people die any more than it ceases to be serious when people laugh." —*George Bernard Shaw*

☺ "When you come to a fork in the road, take it!" —*Yogi Berra*

☺ "If you want to spoil the day for a grouch, give him one of your smiles." —*Unknown*

Whether it's by phone, mail, e-mail, or in person, a touch of humor can be your ally in creating a meeting announcement that nurtures a sense of positive expectation. Figure 3.2 shows how Carol Bailiff sends out friendly meeting reminders to encourage attendance at workshops. Note how she uses a humorous "grabber" and interesting typography to lift people's spirits and bring them to important business with a positive attitude. As Carol says, "Use a fun font for a serious meeting."

Keep in mind that even if you don't feel confident about designing a special invitation or memo, you can always ask another member of your group to do so. And though you can make your meeting announcements more in-viting by adding simple illustrations, quotations, stickers, and fun fonts, don't go crazy. With the ease of computers, it's tempting to put too much stuff on a page. Be sure the message is readable and conveys the who, what, when, where, why, and how of your meeting.

Other Fanciful Touches

Memos and announcements don't have to be boring and predictable. One good-natured secretary pasted chocolate Hershey's Kisses to the usual announcement of a weekly meeting. She enjoyed hearing the sounds of surprise as staff members found the treats in their mailboxes. And they appreciated the fact that someone had done something special for them.

To a potentially stressful memo, one writer simply stapled some tissues. And a fund-raising chair got people to notice the agenda she sent by adding at the bottom: "Chocolate chip cookies and fresh milk will be served." Not only did participants notice the fanciful touch, they came to the meeting in good spirits, ready to work.

Gae was in charge of the major fund-raising event for the alumni group of her professional musical sorority. The goal was to raise $10,000 to provide music scholarships for university students—not an easy task for this group.

The invitation letter for the fund-raising event included a solicitation pledge card for those who could not attend. Gae put the letter and card into regular business envelopes to

Figure 3.2
Fun Fonts

Remember signing up for this?

It was on a cold winter's night . . .

> **#21   Let's Get Spring Fever and READ!**
>
> We'll get together with some 200 or so children's books and sort them by continuum level. If you have some you want included in the "pool," bring them along.
>
> Who?   K–2 teachers
> When?   Mon. April 14, 4:00–7:00 p.m.
>   (light meal provided)
> Where?   Multimedia Conference Room, Balas 2
> By?   District teachers

Well—now it's Spring

so here's your **Reminder**

Please bring books you know and that students read successfully at an independent level. You may wish to bring books connected to your reading series. I will have others to examine.

If you are unable to attend, please call Carol, because **we are serving a light meal.** Thank you.

Note: Adapted by permission of Carol Bailiff and Karen Schulte.

which she affixed preprinted mailing labels. All in all, the envelope looked very plain.

As a piano teacher, Gae often encouraged her students by placing a little sticker on their sheet music to acknowledge their progress. She had a huge collection of humorous, eye-catching stickers with expressions like "Nice job!" "Wow!" or "Good for you!" As she looked over the pile of drab, impersonal solicitations, Gae suddenly had an idea: Put a humorous sticker on each envelope. And she did.

The response to that year's mailing was the best ever. Attendance at the fund raiser was up, and many others sent in contributions. They obviously appreciated the whimsical touch of Gae's stickers on the otherwise plain envelope. It aroused their curiosity and encouraged them to open the letter, which moved them to attend the event or mail in a contribution.

☺   ☺   ☺

If your meeting announcement is going out in an envelope, you don't need to rely on a supply of stickers to gain attention. You could preprint envelopes with a silly message like "Please open before reading!" The object, as with all the suggestions in this chapter, is to make your meeting announcements more inviting without going overboard on the extras.

4

Arrivals and First Impressions

My teacher Ron Lippitt, professor and pioneer in group dynamics, taught that a meeting begins when the very first person arrives; give the early birds something to do while you are waiting for everyone else to arrive.

That "something" can be as simple as reading the agenda, pouring a cup of coffee, making a name tag, completing a survey, greeting the next newcomers, distributing papers, or even arranging the seating. Most people want to be helpful and to feel that their presence makes a difference. *How and if each person is greeted sets the tone for the activity ahead.*

It is easy to overlook planning this part of a meeting. We assume that people will just find each other and comfortably strike up a conversation. Or we assume that they are content passively waiting for the meeting to begin. But feelings of awkwardness and isolation start easily. Providing something for participants to do enhances their sense of comfort and belonging.

Bob Pike, President of Creative Training Techniques Co., tells how he engages people as they arrive in his training meetings (Pike, 1996, p. 14):

> I believe in rewarding people who are on time—not punishing people who are late. A pre-session activity can start 5 to 10 minutes before the formal opening—and run 5 to 10 minutes into the formal time if necessary. But we've still started on time with a value-added activity. The activity could be solving a session-related crossword puzzle or a find-a-word [puzzle].
>
> For example, in many presentations, I'll give participants a find-a-word to work on in [small] groups . . . before the session starts. It will include customized vocabulary for the

session—about 20 words in the list, plus 5 bonus words. These bonus words include my name, the name of the conference, the location of the conference, the key word of the conference theme, and then basic words such as cat, dog, park, and home, etc. I have a small prize for any and all groups that can find all 25 words before the session starts. Later I point out that the bonus words are words that their children can find, and I invite them to take an extra copy for the children. As the children work this, it may be the first time they've ever had a conversation about how Mom and Dad make a living. This is added value![1]

In this chapter, you will find specific ideas for creating an inviting climate as people gather. What you choose to do depends, of course, on the purpose of your meeting, how well people know each other, and, especially, how much time you have. Some ideas are intended for groups that don't know each other well and meet infrequently; others lend themselves to groups that are acquainted and meet regularly. Adapt and modify the activities as necessary.

[1]Used by permission. © Robert W. Pike. All rights reserved.. Phone: 800-383-9210 or 612-829-1954. World Wide Web: http://www.cttbobpike.com.

First Greetings

If your meeting requires registration, seize the opportunity to set an inviting tone. A simple "Welcome!" sign with a touch of humor can lighten the mood. Humorous signs also can be used to direct people to where they need to go. Consider offering small candy bars, mints, or snack crackers on the registration table.

The registration process can be moved into the meeting room itself, if there is space. This allows people to locate their table, leave their coats and belongings, get a snack if one is being served, and register afterwards. Finding a place to sit, by the way, is yet another opportunity for levity. (See the end of the chapter for more on this topic.)

Name Tags: More Than Meets the Eye

Name tags are another wonderful yet often overlooked opportunity to invite participation and create a positive mood as people arrive. But a name tag alone does not start the conversational ball rolling. To get greater mileage and "smileage" from name tags, include something more than a name and title.

Name badges serve three major purposes.

☺ They allow people to address each other by name.

☺ They provide additional information about the person that can stimulate conversation and help people make connections.

☺ They help elicit a smile and create an inviting, friendly, positive tone.

Suppose that in addition to writing your name, where you're from, and your organization, you're asked also to include the name of someone who makes you laugh. You probably start to chuckle as you think of that person. You end up with two names on your badge, and other people can't help asking why you chose the second name. As you talk about your chosen laugh-maker, you again invite smiles. It's hard to talk about someone who makes you laugh without enjoying yourself. And smiles are contagious!

You have at least four choices for using name tags at your meeting.

- You can ask people to create their own.
- You can create them ahead of time.
- You can create partial name tags. That is, you can put the names on and then ask people to add some other information as they arrive.
- You can choose not to use them at all!

Create Their Own Name Tags

You can purchase blank name tags, usually the self-adhesive variety, at any office supply store. As an alternative, you might use index cards with tape or straight pins. Some people even use adding-machine tape: each person tears off enough to make a personalized name tag. You might even try the type of name badge that attaches to a string and hangs around the neck. Don't be shy about using the really large ones so that they can be read from a distance.

Here are some suggestions for adding information to a name tag, guaranteed to promote smiles and conversation. The directions are simple: "On your name tag, please put your own name and . . . "

- *A favorite childhood game or toy.* Maybe it's Monopoly, a Barbie doll, G.I. Joe, little cars and trucks, hide and seek—or playing doctor!
- *The name of someone who makes you laugh.* This could be a comedian, a writer, a friend, or even a relative or colleague.
- *Three numbers that are significant to you, for any reason at all.* One administrator put the numbers 3, 1, and 10 on her name badge. Three is the number of grown children she has; 1 is the number of husbands she has; and 10 is how many years it's been since she last cleaned her kitchen "junk" drawer.
- *A significant personal or professional "first" you've had in the past year.* For example, first grandchild was born; became empty-nesters; got a job promotion; started own company; slept until noon on a weekday.
- *My name is NOT . . .* This can be very inventive. The idea came to me as I was searching for plain, white self-sticking name tags and could find only the ones that proclaimed, "Hello. My Name Is . . . " I thought

to myself, "How silly. Of *course* my name is! Would they really expect me to write what my name is *not?*" Hmm. Possibilities here. What would happen if we each wrote what our *real* name is and also what our name isn't? It's great fun, and I've used this with much success. People write names of family members, celebrities, who they'd *like* to be, who they would *not* like to be, and even the name of their pet. Seinfeld, Erma Bombeck, Aunt Mary, and even Rover have appeared on the name tags. As the choices and reasons are shared, there's always a lot of laughter.

- *Three things about me, two of which are true.* "I'm left-handed; I play the tuba; I grew up in Minneapolis." The attendees are drawn into a guessing game with each conversation: Which is *not* true? They also may discover some common interests.

- *Headlines.* These can be anything at all. Write a caption for your latest accomplishment at work, at home, or in your personal life. Examples: "Mission Accomplished!" "Floor gets washed!" "Kitten adopted." "Fifteen phone calls made." These phrases on a name tag compel others to ask for more details.

- *Something positive about me that people in the room probably can't tell just by looking.* For instance, some people have written, "I'm going to Sweden," "I just bought a new car," "I know all the characters on Sesame Street," "I won an award." These items cover the map. Each person has a license to spread some good news and invite praise and congratulations. Common interests emerge.

- *Something I could use some help with.* This is a great device for promoting conversation *and* solving problems. At a supervisory training session, one participant announced that she had recently moved into a new house. The toilet kept running after it was flushed, and she didn't know how to fix it. Her name tag read, "Running Toilet." She ended up finding several other people in the room who had experienced this situation, and some of them knew what to do about it! Other requests for help might include: "Reliable Car Mechanic," "House Sitter," "Writing," "Job Leads," "Housekeeper," or "Eldercare."

- *Something I know quite a bit about.* As in the previous example, this topic sets the stage for giving and receiving help and for discovering common interests. For example, the name tag might read, "computers," "graphic design," "finding babysitters," "growing roses" "playing the French horn," "getting over stage fright," "nursing homes." It's easy enough for another to ask for more details and perhaps find help that they are seeking. It also is a pleasant way for people to brag a little bit. And especially important, it turns a situation where many of us feel insecure into one that acknowledges our competence.

- *Make a fingerprint.* Have a stamp pad available for participants to add a fingerprint to their name tag. Then they decorate it. It's fun to see the variety of things a fingerprint turns into and the lighthearted conversation that accompanies it.

- *Rename your job in layman's language*. This is a winner in higher education, health care, or any large organization where titles don't begin to convey the tasks involved. So many job names say very little about what the job really entails. An "information system specialist" labeled himself "Help, Help, Help!" He was always receiving frantic calls to fix computer breakdowns.

Create Name Tags Before the Meeting

Preparing name tags in advance has several advantages. It speeds up the registration process, makes people feel expected and welcome, and helps you track who has arrived and who is yet to come.

It's puzzling why the organization's name is twice the size of the attendee's name on some pre-made badges. If we are already at the meeting of an organization, we know its name! Don't let the organization overpower the individual; the participant's name should always be prominent.

At meetings where people are gathered from different parts of the state or country, you might include their city of residence. "Where are you from?" can spark as much interest as "What do you do?" You might even print the name of the city larger than that of the person. It will probably give people more to talk about.

For example, "Oh, you're from Minneapolis. I grew up there!" "You're from Alaska? I've always wanted take a cruise through the fjords." "You're really from New York? So is my cousin! Maybe you know her?" You're off to a stimulating conversation and new connections.

Create Partial Name Tags

Another way to get more mileage from a name tag is to add a humorous or curiosity-provoking cartoon or graphic beforehand. Participants then complete the tag merely by adding their own names.

For example, add a Droodle to the name tag. The late Roger Price, humorist and inventor of the Droodle in the 1950s, called it "a borkley-looking sort of drawing that doesn't make any sense until you know the correct title." Here are some classic Droodles to illustrate the point (Figures 4.1 and 4. 2).

Figure 4.1

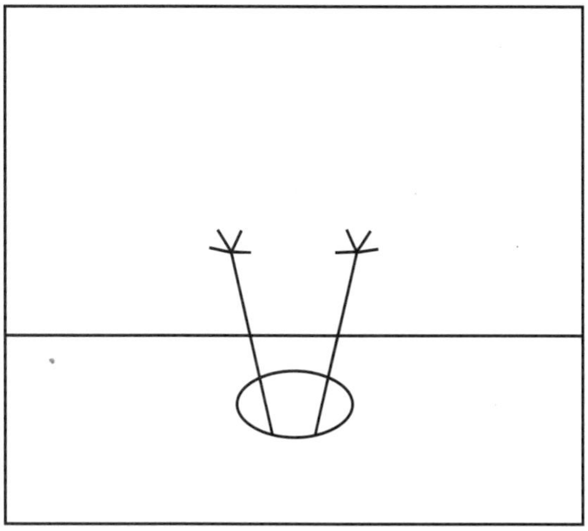

Droodles by Roger Price reprinted by permission of Price Stern Sloan, Inc. from *Classic Droodles*, copyright 1953, © 1981 by Roger Price.

Figure 4.2

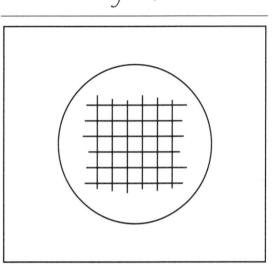

Droodles by Roger Price reprinted by permission of Price Stern Sloan, Inc. from *Classic Droodles*, copyright 1953, © 1981 by Roger Price.

Some think that Figure 4.1 is two palm trees on a desert island, or a gopher with two TV sets. Others see an early bird who caught a very strong worm! Some people have said that Figure 4.2 is an extensive Tic-Tac-Tic-Tac-Tic-Tac-Toe Game or a piece of screen or a piece of fabric under a microscope. Could be. Some people see a plate of spaghetti served by a very, very, very neat person!

You can create your own Droodles or consult the book *Classic Droodles* by Roger Price (1992) for additional ideas. Add one to a name tag and you'll start a massive guessing game. Best of all, there is no right answer; the correct title for a Droodle is only what the viewer happens to see. It's the perfect playful conversation starter.

Droodles also can serve double-duty at a meeting. If at some point you want to create small groups, you can assign people according to the Droodle on their name tag. And of course, the first task they have together is to determine what they think the drawing represents! Since there is no right answer, everyone's ideas count. This leads to creative thinking and laughter. Droodles also make the point that there is no one "right way" to see things; we view the world according to our own experiences and perspectives. We need to honor this in all serious discussions.

Another name tag idea is to "Stick It to 'Em." Children's stickers, cartoons, and other simple graphics can be added to a name tag to trigger conversation and elicit a smile (and form groups later if needed).

Use bright colored papers for your name tags, and let people speculate about the significance of the colors. Later, you can use the colors for assigning groups. Instead of going around the room and numbering off, simply say: "All the blues will meet in the rear left corner by the window." Or, "Create a group of four people. Make sure that no two people have the same color." You can also create the order of participant introductions by name tag color: "Everyone wearing a yellow name tag, please stand up. Tell us your name, where you've come from, and why you're here." You can assign seating arrangements according to the color of the name tags, too.

Consider adding humorous quotations to the name tag. At a lunch-and-learn meeting, the speaker prepared index cards ahead of time with different sayings like "Lord, Grant me patience, but do it NOW!" "A closed mouth gathers no foot!" "Laugh, live, love and be happy!" As people arrived, the speaker greeted them and told each person to select one of the sayings, add his or her name to it, and then wear it as a name badge. As they did so, they couldn't help remarking to one another, "Oh yeah, this is ME!" It immediately created something to talk about.

You might want to create a badge that says, "Hello, my name is _____ and I _____." On this name badge, each person fills in the blanks as he or she likes. You may want to post a sign suggesting the possible verbs to follow "I", such as *am, was, will be, want to, have to, like to, think that, know, do, did, will do, have, had, will have, see, saw, will see, hate to,* or *don't like.* The rest is up to the participants.

Skip the Name Tags!

If the people at your meeting all know each other pretty well, there's probably no need for a name tag. But if you want to create a climate that promotes participation and productivity, consider additional activities that help create a positive meeting climate, such as interactive surveys.

Interactive Surveys

Interactive surveys go by the name of "ice breakers," "warm-ups," and "energizers."

Whatever the language, enlisting people in an interactive survey when they arrive serves three functions:

☺ It gives them something meaningful and fun to do.

☺ It promotes a connection with others in the room in pleasant, safe ways.

☺ It can introduce the content of the meeting.

Some great ice breakers are the Human Treasure Hunt, Human Bingo, and Unusual Research.

Special Human Treasure Hunt

A "Human Treasure Hunt" consists of 10–15 items on a sheet of paper that require participants to interact with each other. It is impossible to complete the Hunt without talking to someone else. Questions such as the following can be included:

- Find someone who has a birthday in the same month as yours.
- Find someone who can recite the alphabet backwards.
- Find someone who has a hole in their sock.
- Find someone who knows the name of the founder of this organization.
- Find someone who hates filling out these kinds of forms!

See Figure 4.3 (on next page) for a sample Treasure Hunt activity.

Figure 4.3
—————————— *A Special Ho-Ho Treasure Hunt* ——————————

Directions: Talk to people in this room and find someone who fits each of the descriptions. **Using a name only once,** write it on the appropriate line. When you finish, claim your prize from the presenter.

 **Find someone in this room who:**

1. Is happy to have you use their name here on the **first line.** _____

2. Has a **birthday** in the same month as yours. _____

3. Likes **prune juice.** _____

4. Can name **two** positive things that **humor and laughter** do for us at work.

   _____

5. Remembers eating an **unusual food combination** in their youth. (Find out what it was.) _____

6. Can recite the **alphabet** backwards. _____

7. Has an idea for **making their workplace a little more fun.** _____

8. **Doesn't feel like doing this activity right now.** _____

9. You have **never met** before. (Do something about that.) _____

10. Finally **accomplished something** they've been meaning to get around to doing. (Congratulate them!) _____

11. Has a **silly habit**—like biting the ends off the hot dog, playing their CDs in alphabetical order, keeping their wastebaskets empty all the time. _____

12. Has a **hole** in their sock. _____

13. Will tell you what they think an **"Inverse Paranoid"** is. _____

Sometimes you can gather specific tidbits about the group members ahead of time and then customize the Treasure Hunt based on those items. One couple created a Treasure Hunt for their wedding guests. As people visited at the reception, they searched for answers to such items as "someone who knew Katie in the 3rd grade," "someone who came here from Hawaii," "someone who was Mark's roommate in college." Be sure to recognize or award prizes to people who complete the hunt. More ideas for Treasure Hunt questions can be found in Appendix A.

Human Bingo

One variation of a Treasure Hunt is done on a "Bingo" form with anywhere from 16 to 25 squares. The participant's mission is to find people who fit the descriptions in the boxes. For example, "A person wearing mismatched socks." "Someone who likes prune juice." "Born in the same month as you." "Can name all of their elementary schoolteachers." "Knows how this company got its name." When someone gets a Bingo, you can stop, or the game can continue until the entire page is filled. See Figure 4.4 (on next page) for a sample Human Bingo form.

Before long, group members begin to collaborate, sharing names they've captured with each other. "Dennis owns his own business; you can put his name in the 'self-employed' box." "Rachel was a Campfire Girl." People are genuinely learning new and fun things about each other. You can emphasize that you want people to meet one another; but if they get creative and share names, don't penalize them. The objective is to have fun.

Unusual Research

On some occasions, you may want to provide a series of questions for people to "research" as they gather for the meeting. These can be whimsical questions, or they may be related to key issues the meeting will address. Each person receives a sheet of paper with two or three different questions on it. Their task is to ask the question of as many people as they can before the meeting comes to order.

At some point early in the meeting, the leader then asks for a report of what was learned. This always produces chuckles, as well as interesting results. And it engages everyone.

At an association dinner meeting where I was the speaker, I gave participants a handout with the following:

> You are invited to participate in some fascinating "research" for tonight's meeting. Findings will be shared later in the program. Your research questions (should you choose to accept them) are:
>
> • How many people can you find here tonight who have never been to a meeting of this group before?
>
> • How many people can you find here tonight who remember some enjoyable toys or games they played when they were younger?

Figure 4.4
— *Human Bingo* —

Directions: Try to fill in as many spaces as you can. You may use one person's name only twice. SMILE!

A person whose birthday is in the same month as yours.	Someone who has a hole in their sock!	Who was a Boy or Girl Scout in their youth?	This person has a hobby. (Find out what it is.)	Someone who wears some item of clothing the same size as you do.
Someone who played with the same childhood toy or game as you did.	Who knows the names of all 50 state capitals?	A person whose eyes are a different color from yours.	Someone who is very excited about what he or she is doing these days.	A person who could use a hug right now. (Give him or her one, if you'd like.)
Who traveled more miles than you did to get to this meeting?	Someone in here who you've not met before. (Do something about that.)	YOUR OWN NAME GOES RIGHT HERE.	Who can recited the alphabet backwards? (Check it out!)	Someone who likes the same comedian as you do.
Who intentionally plans for ways to add humor and laughter to their work life?	A person who plays a musical instrument.	A person whose hand is about the same size as yours.	A person who carries something in his or her wallet, purse, or briefcase that makes the person chuckle, smile, or laugh.	Someone whose job title or primary responsibility is different from yours.
Who can identify at least two benefits of humor in our lives? (What are they?)	Someone who reads "Pot Shots" by Ashleigh Brilliant.	Someone who likes prune juice.	The last digit of your home phone number: Who in here has the same one?	Anyone's name that you haven't used can be put in here!

Using the same introductory sentence, I ted the following two questions on a differ-t sheet of paper:

- How many people can you find here tonight who were born in the same month as you were?
- How many people can you find here tonight who have attended either a workshop, conference, or speech about the topic of humor in the past year?

On yet another sheet, with the same intro-duction, were two more questions. In total, there were five different pages, each with two questions. I had made 6 copies of each one (30 in all). As participants arrived, I in-vited them to participate, and the conversa-tions became very lively. The questions are similar to those on the Treasure Hunt and Bingo. It's the format and directions that are different.

A Word of Caution

I have found that when getting-acquainted ac-tivities are viewed as games, or add-ons, with no apparent relationship to the purpose of the meeting, they lose their power. It's important to integrate the results of the activity into the meeting.

For example, after people complete a Treasure Hunt, ask some questions about it: "Who finished the whole thing?" This allows you to give a prize or at least to acknowledge the efforts of your participants. "What items

do you need some help with?" This allows you to expand on any of the more interesting tidbits and then segue into the main purpose of your meeting. It also allows people to discover things about each other that they probably didn't know earlier. And it can put them at ease.

In addition, some items on the Treasure Hunt can relate to an issue that will be ad-dressed at the meeting, such as "Find someone who has an idea for a fund-raising project" or "Find a person who would be happy to write an article for the newsletter."

Finding a Place to Sit

Have you ever had the experience of scanning a room, searching for someone you know will be a good table partner? The quandary: Do you sit with someone safe—whom you know well—or should you expand your horizons and meet new people? But what if they don't want to talk with you? What if it turns out that they are boring? Why risk it? The more you think about it, the more foolish you feel for attaching so much importance to what should be a simple decision.

The seemingly simple choice of where to sit can cause momentary tension or high anxi-ety for some meeting-goers. It becomes a par-ticularly important decision at an interactive gathering such as a workshop, a lunch or din-ner meeting, a planning meeting, or a start-of-the-year retreat. It's most definitely important at a social gathering where place cards have not been assigned.

Reserved Tables

As a meeting planner, you can help ease the tension and facilitate the seating by creating playful "Reserved for . . . " signs.

One newly formed health-care organization had a day-long meeting of all their managers and directors. The 150 attendees, from four major hospitals, gathered to hear from the leaders about changes ahead in the health-care system and what effects they would have on each of the other units. People were apprehensive about potential budget cuts and service reductions. Some were anxious about the status of their own jobs.

The meeting planners knew that the day needed some fun if the participants were going to be able to openly discuss their concerns. They wanted people from the different hospitals to mingle and share their different perspectives. The day was to be one of reports, questions, and responses. The leaders chose this format because they wanted everyone to hear the same information at the same time and place. They wanted to share their vision, be reassuring, and learn the concerns of the various departments.

People arrived and were directed to write out a name tag. They added the sticky colored dot designated to represent their own hospital before entering the large ballroom, arranged with round tables, each accommodating six chairs. No more than two people from any one hospital were to be seated at the same table.

On each table was a "reserved" sign, purposely created to invite a smile and ease the tension (see Figure 4.5). For example, there were tables reserved for meeting-goers who:

Figure 4.5

Reserved for chocoholics

Reserved for people who have a hard time making decisions

- can sing "My Bonnie Lies Over the Ocean"
- had a hole in their sock yesterday
- like to eat prunes
- can juggle and do magic acts
- can't spell potato
- eat breakfast every morning
- can recite a nursery rhyme
- can't sing in tune
- don't know how they got their first name
- no longer have birthdays
- have ever worn mismatched shoes to work
- could run a better meeting
- like to sit at square tables
- don't like meetings like this
- like to be alone
- play musical instruments
- belong or belonged to a PTO
- are really excited to be here

- are great listeners but prefer to talk
- have hidden talents
- can sing in harmony
- would rather be golfing
- have a hole in their sock
- sing in the shower
- were Girl or Boy Scouts
- brush and floss after every meal
- have naturally straight hair
- like people
- never fall asleep at meetings like this
- have a birthday in the merry month of May
- can hum the theme song from "Gilligan's Island"
- do not have a fax machine in their car
- love jelly beans
- still have their appendix
- are chocoholics
- would rather be shopping in New York

The laughter in the room was immediate. People had fun as they looked around for "their" spot and listened to the strains of a Sousa March over the loudspeakers.

Newspaper Cartoons

You can also help people to comfortably find a place to sit by using newspaper cartoons, such as Ziggy, Dilbert, or The Far Side; colored slips of paper; Droodles; or sayings or expressions. People are given one as they enter the room, and then they find their seats according to your directions. For example, "Everyone who has a Ziggy cartoon, sit together. Everyone with a Far Side, sit together. Everyone with a Dilbert, sit together." Then when they sit, their first task is to compare cartoons. This invites instant smiles and connections through laughter.

The primary object of incorporating fun activities as people gather at a meeting is to create a spirit of involvement and cooperation. If people are relaxed and engaged, they can more easily make the transition from "then" to "now."

Again, your actual decision about arrival activities is very much determined by the meeting's purpose, how well the people know each other, the space available, and the amount of time you have. You wouldn't play Human Bingo before a board meeting, nor would you likely use name tags at a weekly staff meeting—or would you? These ideas can be dynamite at a dinner meeting, family reunion, or an annual educators' con-ference. Whatever you choose, make sure that it enhances your meeting and that every-one has an opportunity to be involved if they want.

5

Look Who's Here!
Introducing Participants

The dinner part of the monthly association meeting was over, and dessert had been cleared. There were about 25 people, seated at four round tables. Everyone turned their attention to the program chair as she stepped up to the podium.

"I'd like to welcome you all to tonight's meeting," she began. "We have quite a few announcements to make before our speaker starts, so to save time, we're just going to have the new people introduce themselves. Why don't you start, yes, you at this first table."

Does this sound familiar?

Unfortunately, it is a perfect example of unintentionally sending thoughtless messages to an audience. The program chair was implying that the *people* at the meeting were less important than the program (and this was supposed to be a networking meeting!). Newcomers were put on the spot. The regulars were denied the opportunity to learn who else was in the room, and they wouldn't get the chance to introduce themselves to the newcomers.

One respected, long-time member of this organization couldn't help himself. He stood up and exclaimed, "You mean you're not going to have the old-timers introduce themselves as well? I haven't been here for a long time, and I'd like to know who is at the other tables. This is a group that encourages networking!"

The program chair reluctantly agreed: "Well, if we have time after the new people are introduced, I guess we could do that."

As it turned out, there was enough time. The introductions took less than 10 minutes. But unfortunately (and unnecessarily), the tone had been charged negatively. And to add further salt to the wound, the evening speaker was not very good.

Self-introductions *are* an important part of a meeting. They're not a throw-away item;

they're actually a perfect opportunity to create camaraderie, enhance the sense of shared purpose, and invite a little levity. But like every other part of a meeting, they need to be planned.

Why Are Introductions So Important?

Have you ever heard a leader say, "First of all, let's go around the room. Everyone tell us your name, what you do, and a little about yourself." How do you feel when you hear those directions? If you're like many people, you immediately tense up. Your pulse quickens; your palms get sweaty. Your mind races, frantically wondering, "Omigosh! What should I say?"

If you're a meeting planner, you may be thinking, "I don't want to make people uncomfortable, but I want everyone to know who's here." For many people, however, the moments before speaking their name are filled with panic. "Where *do* I work? What do I *do*?? And what *else* am I supposed to mention? I can't think!" Rehearsing our own introduction, we become so preoccupied figuring out what to include that we don't hear a thing anyone before us has said. That kind of defeats the purpose, doesn't it?

Though self-introductions can be challenging, they're vital to the program. It's just good manners and common courtesy to introduce people to one another. Introductions also can

☺ make everyone feel welcome

☺ give all participants a sense of who's there and why and where they fit in

☺ increase the knowledge people have of one another

☺ build a sense of togetherness

☺ identify group resources

☺ find out who needs help with what

☺ help people tune in to the task of the meeting instead of being distracted by wondering, "Who is that over there?"

The way you choose to handle introductions can build unity or create discomfort. If it causes discomfort, or does not advance the goals of the meeting, then of course the purpose has been defeated. Fortunately, there are ways to ease the tension generated by the seemingly simple act of stating our names. With a little planning, you can use introductions to produce an energetic, focused meeting climate.

Important Considerations

Meeting planners need to consider four important questions:

• What do you want people to say about themselves?

• In what order should they speak?

• How long should they talk?

• How much time can you allow for the entire introduction process?

The answers to these questions, of course, are interrelated. How much time you can allow affects the kind of information you ask people to disclose and even the sequence of speaking. And how much time you allot is determined by the purpose of your meeting.

It's hard to say how long introductions should be. For example, if you have only five minutes to use, you might ask the group questions like these: "How many of you have been here before? Who knows all the other people in the room? Who likes to eat peanut-butter and jelly sandwiches?" If you have a longer time, each person can be introduced individually.

Remember, too, that while structured introductions usually occur at the beginning of a meeting, they can continue throughout; we are continually letting people know things about ourselves, whether we intend to or not.

Now that you see why introductions should be included, how can you make them a positive experience? Following are suggestions for:

- What people can say about themselves.
- New ways to determine the order of who speaks first so you're not always "going around the room" or "up and down the rows."
- Choosing what you'll do, based on important criteria.

More Than a Name

When we gather at a meeting, what do we want to know about each other besides our names? Most meeting participants have lots of unasked questions about the others in the group. You can engage their help at the begin-

ning of the meeting by asking them to identify some of the things they'd like to know about each other. You can use those questions, as well as some you've prepared beforehand, such as:

- How long have you been in this organization?
- What do you remember about your first day on the job?
- What do you remember about your first meeting?
- Why are you here today?

See Appendix A for even more ideas about how what people can say about themselves during an introduction.

Who Starts?

The tension builds as you see it coming. The introductions began on the first row, far left, and are snaking their way toward you. You calculate how long before it's your turn. Thirteen more people before you have to speak. Now six. Why are you so nervous? It's a simple law of psychology. When we are concentrating very hard on something that is usually second nature to us, it can suddenly become more difficult to remember. Try explaining to a new driver exactly how to exert the right amount of pressure on the accelerator. Or introduce your best friend to the mayor of your city. (In the presence of a dignitary, it is not uncommon to momentarily forget something you know very well, like your best friend's name.) When we're under pressure to speak, we often become anxious, even about something as simple as stating our name.

Eliminate anxiety. How can you avoid this anxiety? Eliminate the anticipation. Scrap the predictable process of going up and down the rows or around the tables. Instead, introduce people by categories.

For example, "If you've belonged to this organization 10 years or more, stand up (or wave your hand)." After several people are standing (or waving—always be sensitive to people who either can't stand or are uncomfortable with standing), welcome them in random order. "Now, tell us your name and when you joined, and one thing your remember about your first meeting."

Continue, "If you've belonged to this organization 5–10 years, stand, tell us your name and when you joined, and one thing you remember about your first meeting." Continue until you've come to the newest members, asking them, "What do you remember about your entry into this room?"

An advantage to this method is that people have a chance to see who's been around a while, and the newcomers get a sense of what's appropriate to say. And above all, everyone is introduced comfortably.

In smaller meetings with short time frames, going around the table is probably efficient and adequate, as in a meeting where everyone knows each other but the two new members. Even in these kinds of meetings, however, you can include some questions that help people tune in to the business in a pleasant and comfortable way.

Following are some more ways that you can eliminate "going around the room" and facilitate introductions in a more comfortable manner. Adapt them to suit your own setting.

Check out the birthdays. In any group of 25 or more people, there is a good chance that at least two people will share the same birth month and day (though usually not the year). So, in the interest of "research," find out how many pairs are in your particular group. This kind of "study" works well with groups of 10 to 100.

You can start with the current month and then skip around the calendar so that no one is too busy anticipating their turn. "When I call your month, please stand up." Standing up puts energy into the room. It changes the pace and allows people to see each other. And usually at least two people will be standing at the same time, so it's not intimidating. Plus, birthdays become the most important item at the moment; people are not so nervous when they're standing up for this kind of a reason. Of course, if someone is unable to stand, a simple wave of the hand will do.

Now, direct each of those standing to call out their birthdate. It's amazing to see how people really listen to this! And they get *very* excited when there is a pair. Clapping and cheering erupt. Sometimes people become so excited that they run over and hug each other! And you'll also hear comments like "That's my daughter's birthday!" This exercise invariably causes laughter and raises spirits.

By the way, I also use this opportunity to provide a small prize. When there is a pair (or more) of birthdays, I give the lucky "winners" the special "free ticket" in Figure 5.1.

Continue, "As long as you're standing, tell us your name, where you're from, and what you wrote on your name tag." People who have participated in this activity report that they are much more comfortable introducing themselves. For that moment, their birthday is what's most important; the name is secondary. Hence, it's easier to remember what to say. And since people have been laughing together, they are more comfortable and less nervous speaking to the group.

In the interest of "science," appoint one or two members of the group to keep track of the number of pairs, or even triplets. Find out which is the most popular month, which is the least popular, which date recurs most often, which month has no birthdays, and any other items of significance. This keeps everyone attentive and involved. You can also ask, "How many of you noticed that someone in here has a birthday on the same day as your mother, father, sister, brothers, spouse, or kids? Now, what does this say about the group?" Probably not much except that everyone has a birthday!

Figure 5.1

FREE TICKET

This is a Free Ticket.
It isn't good for anything. It's just free!

"Putting Humor to Work"
Speeches • Workshops • Consultations
SHEILA FEIGELSON, Ph.D.

P.O. Box 7262
Ann Arbor,
MI 48107

HappyF@aol.com

© 1992

Use "Unusual Research." Following are some variations on the "research" theme.

- *Follow the order of vowels.* "Think of the first vowel in your first name: *a, e, i, o,* or *u,* and sometimes *y.* Which do you think is most popular? Okay. Let's check it out." Then just call out the vowel, people stand, do a quick count, and each person introduces himself or herself.
- *Go by the order of the last digit of the home phone number.* "Which do you think is most popular?" Then call a digit, people stand, count them, and make introductions. Again, focusing on something other than self helps to reduce the stress associated with saying our name and other information about us.
- *Use street names.* "Anyone who spent some of their childhood on a street that began with A, tell us the name of your street and your own name. Now, who began on a street starting with B?" Some people may discover someone who grew up in their own neighborhood. And it's amazing to see how many different cities have the same street names. You might ask people to use their current address rather than a former one as a way to help people discover neighbors.

All these devices allow people to relate in a lighthearted way and break the monotony and predictability of going around the room. Even more important, they put people at ease. Participants stay interested, alert, and they have fun. A positive tone is created early in the meeting.

There is one main point to consider as you plan introductions: What do people want to know about each other? Often it's information that can help us connect with one another: where we're from; where we have lived; what we do, or did, for a living; or our personal interests. On some level, whenever we meet new people, we're always listening for, "What's interesting about that person? What do we have in common? How can we serve each other?"

Criteria to Remember

If you are the person managing introductions, keep the following caveats in mind.

- *What is the purpose of the meeting?* Obviously you wouldn't call out birthdays at an annual stockholders meeting. But it could work well for an association luncheon or dinner meeting, a weekend retreat, a reunion, a PTA group, Scouts, or a celebration.
- *How well acquainted are the people with each other?* If the meeting participants don't know each other at all, introductions are certainly in order. If, on the other hand, participants frequently see each other and have worked together over a long period, they don't need name tags or self-introductions. However, you can still launch the meeting with a round of information-gathering that grabs people's attention and fosters participation. A teaching staff, for example, begins its biweekly staff meetings with a quick round of "anything positive that has happened since

we last met." Each person keeps it short: a headline, or a quick sentence or two, but no lengthy anecdotes. It can be work- or home-related, such as "I read a great book" or "We have a new grandchild." The teller gets a chance to relive a pleasant experience and earn praise and congratulations. Thus, the meeting always starts on a positive note.

- *How much time is available?* Whether it's a half-hour team meeting, an evening dinner gathering, or a three-day retreat, the primary structure of the meeting is the same: people arrive, they conduct their business, and they leave. No matter how long or short the meeting, people need a moment to transition into the task at hand. Introductions serve that purpose.

The amount of time you allot to introductions may consume anywhere from five minutes to an hour. It depends on your agenda. A possible formula might be 10 to 15 percent of your allotted meeting time for some kind of organized introduction activity. Remember that the primary purpose is to safely increase the knowledge that people have one of the other.

Often, meetings don't go well because we focus on the agenda and forget about the people who are addressing the issues. Striking a balance between task and people is always challenging. Next to reaching consensus or closure, it may be *the* greatest challenge a meeting leader faces.

Remember, too, that there are ways for people to get to know each other better during the course of the meeting as well. Not all introductions have to take place at the beginning.

- *How many people are at the meeting?* The size of the group certainly influences your choice of introduction activity. What works around a conference table won't fly in an auditorium. You can't stage an introduction marathon for hundreds of people. But, even in a very large group, you can give people the feeling of being acquainted. Here's a simple activity: Ask people in pairs to tell each other about their past 24 hours. You'll be amazed to hear the laughter that this generates. Within two minutes, everyone has had a chance to speak, learn something about one other person, and feel acquainted.

Choose a few questions that the entire audience can respond to: "Raise your right hand if your workload sometimes drives you crazy. Raise your left hand if you have felt any stress in the past week. Now raise both hands if you could use a good laugh this morning!"

The objective is to let participants feel valued and welcome. It's more than just saying, "I'm really glad you came." Reinforce that phrase by following it with "because": "I'm glad you came because today we are going to be talking about some of the best ways to improve morale and have fun in our organization!"

Special Situations: A Very Large Group

How often do you make presentations at meetings of thousands of people? Master trainer

Bob Pike, President of Creative Training Techniques Inc., periodically has such opportunities as he travels the world helping trainers become better at their jobs.

At the 1996 international conference of the American Society of Training and Development (ASTD), Pike used an interactive, participant-honoring opening as he addressed an audience of 2,600 people. He describes how he began his presentation:

"This is the ASTD international conference. Many of you speak a language other than English. I'd like you to get a group of five or six people together in at least two rows. I'll give you 30 seconds to put your group together. (I paused, then continued.) As a group, I'd like you to brainstorm and come up with your guess as to the 10 languages most widely spoken in the world. You have 90 seconds to do this. Give it your best. Go." (At the end of 90 seconds, I continued.)

"If you can hear my voice, clap once (I clapped once). If you can hear my voice, clap twice (I clapped twice). If you can hear my voice, clap three times." (I clapped three times. By this time I had everybody refocused on me for the next instruction.)

"Great. I'd like some groups to volunteer one guess as to one of the languages in the top 10. My source, by the way (and I held it up), is *The Top Ten of Everything for 1996*."

I then took guesses. If a guess was correct—such as English—I'd say, "That's right. It's No. 2." Or Japanese: "That's right; it's No. 10." I'd also give the number of people that spoke the language. Several guesses were not in the top 10, so I'd say, "French—great language, but not in the top 10."

Two of the languages were little known to the participants as a whole. When people volunteered them as guesses, there was laughter, which quickly stopped when I said, "Bengali, that's right. It's No. 7."

Then I started at No. 1—Chinese—and asked all those who spoke Chinese to stand. We gave them a round of applause. We continued for English and so on through the top 10. Every language was represented.

Then I asked, "What other languages are represented?" As people volunteered languages, I repeated them and had those that spoke them stand to be applauded.

I then talked about the dangers of assumptions and prejudging, and the importance of having an open mind and used that as a springboard into the rest of my presentation. I had my audience with me, in part because I acknowledged and honored them. I'll use the same opening at an international conference in Korea this month with 8,000 attendees from 110 countries" (Pike, 1996, pp. 12–13).[1]

---

[1]Used by permission. © Robert W. Pike. All rights reserved.. Phone: 800-383-9210 or 612-829-1954. World Wide Web: http://www.cttbobpike.com.

The logistics of the room affects the choice of introduction plans, particularly for very large gatherings. What is the room arrangement? If the room is too large for people to hear one another or have eye contact, don't bother to have introductions from the floor. A portable microphone could help, but it might be cumbersome to pass during random introductions.

The choice of what you do also is affected by seating arrangements. If people are seated around a table, great. No need to stand or be formal. But if they can't see one another, they should stand up. The person leading the introduction activities—the emcee—creates comfort by selecting what else people should say besides their names.

☺   ☺   ☺

The leader's demeanor can make or break the introduction process. My advice is to do what you are comfortable with. If you're the meeting leader and you're not at ease with this part of the meeting, invite another participant to facilitate it. Just keep in mind that common courtesy suggests we somehow allow time for our meeting participants to meet and greet one another. And the process of introducing group members is just one more opportunity to invite a smile and, even more important, create a climate of productive participation.

6

As the Meeting Moves: Print, Props, and Visual Aids

In previous chapters, we looked at ways to create an engaging and productive meeting climate as participants receive the meeting announcement, arrive at the meeting place, and are introduced. But perhaps the easiest way to invite laughter at a meeting—without asking participants to do anything at all—is through the tangible, visible items in the room. The mere presence of novelties like special printed materials, displays, or props can evoke a chuckle from attendees.

Lightening Up the Agenda (and Other Printed Matter)

Most effective meetings have agendas. Some groups develop an agenda on the spot. Some agendas are written on flipchart paper or a chalkboard for all to see. But usually the agenda is printed on standard typing paper and distributed to participants. Some leaders send out these agendas ahead of time; others distribute them at the meeting itself. Regardless of how and when the agenda is determined and communicated, it is important to have one. Basically, people want an agenda so that they know what to expect.

A printed agenda provides another opportunity to lighten up your gathering with simple clip art, cartoons, or other whimsical drawings and quotes. Since we are such a visual society—and we are inundated with paper—a few special touches can make your printed matter stand out from the pack. Here are some possibilities for lightening up the printed agenda:

- Include witty sayings and quotes.
- Try using acronyms like the word L-A-U-G-H as the agenda. For example:

Look at some ideas.
Answer Questions.
Understand new procedures.
Go for it.
How we will know we've succeeded.

- List each item in the form of a question: "How in the world are we going to get this job done anyhow?!"
- Label the space at the bottom, "For Doodling Only!"
- Put the word "Surprise" on the agenda—and be sure to include one!
- Include some irrelevant item just for a change of pace. For example, "Bananas on sale this week" or "The sun rises in the East."
- Put "adjournment" as the first item. Have you ever noticed that people are more creative and energetic *after* a meeting is adjourned? Why not start the meeting with the ending?
- Put times by each item, and be *very* specific. You can even use military time to exaggerate the point: 18:36:25–20:36:27.
- Create a random agenda. List each agenda item on a strip of paper. Place them into a container. At the meeting, let the participants pull a slip out, one at a time, then deal with each item.
- Of course, you can always decorate your agenda with a bit of lighthearted artwork.

Getting People to Read Minutes, Reports, and Summaries

A frequent complaint is that people don't read materials sent to them before a meeting.

To remedy this, one corresponding secretary attached a note: "See if you can find the mistake in these minutes." Several people did!

Generally, minutes or summaries are written after the meeting is over. Christeen Holdwick, a hospital administrator who appreciates the value of playfulness, decided to have fun with her task force of eight health-care colleagues. The group had been meeting regularly for more than three months, working on a special project for the hospital. At each group gathering, they received minutes of the previous meeting. These minutes always followed the same format: a statement of the topic under consideration, followed by highlights of the discussion, followed by actions that were to be taken between meetings. Chris noticed that the minutes were all beginning to sound alike.

One day, she wrote up the meeting's minutes *before* it began. And she started the meeting by saying, "Do you want to know what we did at today's meeting? Here are the minutes." She presented the report as it was always written up: topic, discussion, action. Her colleagues appreciated her sense of fun and had a good laugh. More striking was the fact that she predicted the meeting minutes quite accurately! In the end, much was accomplished that day.

Playful Props and Visual Aids

You can inject humor into meetings in many ways by using props and visual aids. Here are some of my favorites.

Figure 6.1

POT-SHOTS NO. 184

APPRECIATE ME NOW

and avoid the rush

APPRECIATION HOURS

© BRILLIANT ENTERPRISES 1970

Ashleigh Brilliant

Reprinted by permission of Ashleigh Brilliant. Copyright © 1970 by Ashleigh Brilliant.

Playful Parasols

You're probably familiar with the little parasols that sometimes decorate a drink—the ones that create an irresistible urge to twirl them between your thumb and forefinger. At one meeting, nine planning committee members arrived to find one of these little trinkets at each of their places. Why were they there?

The meeting chair explained that she wanted to first spark people's curiosity and then provide them something to fiddle with as they were "fiddling" with ideas for their next event. She knew that a surprise toy would help put everyone in a positive frame of mind to contribute. And it did.

An On-Target Arrow

The beginning of the fall semester was always the busiest time of year for the campus bookstore. Students in the long lines were impatient. They gasped as they learned the price of their books. The sales floor was understaffed, and everyone was working long hours. The manager knew there was a lot of stress and decided to do something about it.

Figure 6.2

©ASHLEIGH BRILLIANT 1989.   POT-SHOTS NO. 4934.

SPECIAL OFFER:

Ashleigh
Brilliant
SANTA BARBARA

BUY ONE
FOR TWICE THE PRICE,
AND GET
ANOTHER ONE
FREE!

Reprinted by permission of Ashleigh Brilliant. Copyright © 1989 by Ashleigh Brilliant.

At the daily meeting the next morning, the manager walked in wearing one of those toy arrows that fits over your head and appears to be going right through it. "I don't know about you," he said, "but I have the strangest headache. This pace is killing me!"

With that as the introduction, the employees laughed and relaxed a bit. They went on to identify their own concerns about what was going on, along with some ways to manage them. They left the meeting in a better frame of mind, recognizing that their manager also felt the pressure of that particular week.

And if he could laugh at himself, perhaps they could, too.

Stimulating Postcards

Pay attention to the things that make you smile: cartoons, quips, illustrations, trinkets. Collect and share them with others. I carry "Pot Shots" postcards by Ashleigh Brilliant in my calendar (Figures 6.1–6.3). Brilliant (his real name) is the creator of thousands of clever epigrams, which he says "are never, under my strict rules, longer than 17 words, and are carefully constructed to carry the

Figure 6.3

Reprinted by permission of Ashleigh Brilliant. Copyright © 1981 by Ashleigh Brilliant.

most weight for the least freight." Among my favorites are the cards shown here.

While waiting for a meeting to begin, I like to set a couple of these cards by my place. Someone nearby invariably notices, and that invites a pleasant exchange, just enough to spark a smile and lighten the mood. See the Resources section for a list of books with Brilliant's more than 5,000 other sayings.

Taking Aim

The school board had voted to institute new requirements for high school graduation and to create new programs at various schools.

The superintendent and his staff had the difficult task of explaining to the public what was going to happen, as well as allaying concerns.

Change doesn't come easily to many people. The parents who had come to the community meeting were anxious, and they wanted good explanations for the decisions. One school official, known for his good humor, arrived at the meeting wearing a sandwich board. A target was painted on each side. Convening the meeting, he stepped to the microphone and announced, "I know you have lots of shots you want to sling at us, so feel free to use the next 20 minutes to shoot your arrows. See how many hit the bull's eye!"

The surprised audience laughed, many hurled their verbal "arrows," and then they settled down and listened to what the administrators had to say. Not all in the audience were won over to the new plan, but they certainly felt better knowing that their concerns were acknowledged—and that the administrator had a sense of humor.

Other Lighthearted Laugh-Getters

There are endless ways to add a little humor to a meeting. For example, budgets are always a challenge. At one annual budget meeting, several managers had to vie for funds for the coming year. Of course, each manager wanted as large a slice of the "pie" as possible. One scored points by wearing a pig-snout mask. Although he didn't get the funds that he requested, he helped his colleagues laugh, and that was rewarding in itself.

To make some serious points, training director Warren Cohen often uses wind-up toys. One time he wound up a toy alligator, set it on the table, and let it go. As it was moving, he said to the group, "Like the alligator, we have to get from here to there." Have you ever seen a set of wind-up chattering teeth? Warren likes to use it as a signal for "time-out."

In the middle of several slides or transparencies, insert an unrelated item, like a tax return, cartoon, or a quote. A researcher I know inserts a vacation photo of his son on waterskis amid the slides of bar charts and other scientific data. The juxtaposition catches his audience off guard and wakes them up to pay attention. It also gives him a chance to show his human side to the audience.

☺   ☺   ☺

These kinds of safe surprises are nearly foolproof for adding levity to a meeting. Just be certain your surprise is truly fun, in good taste, and presented with a sense of timing. Your selections should be enjoyable attention-getters and tension-relievers that enhance—rather than detract from—the meeting. As a by-product, you'll find that when you look for these treats, you'll get double the chuckle: one for yourself and another for those with whom you share them.

7

Dividing into smaller Groups

In some meetings, there are times when you want to create smaller subgroups to discuss an idea, to brainstorm for new ideas, or to get better acquainted. However, a seemingly innocent direction like "Everyone get into groups of three" can raise the pulse rate of even the most relaxed meeting-goer. Most everyone will wonder: "Who should I choose? Will someone choose me? How do I know if I want to have him or her as a partner? How long will we be working together?"

At most meetings, we tend to sit with people we know. It's comfortable. But sometimes we need to meet new people and hear what others we don't know are doing and thinking. Dividing into subgroups is not only useful— it can be essential to the success of a meeting. This is especially true when you want participants to

☺ meet new people, as in a networking meeting;

☺ brainstorm or discuss ideas, as in a decision-making or learning meeting; or

☺ find a place to sit, as at a celebration where a meal is being served.

I once was part of a committee planning a women's health conference. Generally, our meetings were quite productive, but on one occasion we seemed to be going nowhere. Our task was to identify topics for smaller discussion sessions and to think about what kinds of questions should be addressed in each of them. We were totally stuck. No new ideas emerged.

The 10 of us decided to divide into smaller groupings to see if that might generate more thoughts. When we reconvened after just 15 minutes, it was amazing to see how creative and revitalized we had become. Just by changing the groupings, pace, and location, we got the wheels turning again. The change helped us to see things from a different perspective and to come up with many more ideas.

There is something about talking in smaller groups that allows for more expression; it also allows more people to be talking at the same time. As the facilitator, you can help meeting participants subdivide into groups in light-hearted ways that will ease the tension of mixing with unfamiliar faces. This chapter describes several ways to pair off or organize smaller groups without raising anyone's anxiety level.

Creating Small Groups with Ease

In the book *Playfair*, authors Matt Weinstein and Joel Goodman (1980) offer an array of lighthearted ideas for dividing large groups into smaller ones. For example, ask participants to take out a $1, $5, or $10 bill. (The size of the currency does not matter.) Then ask them to look at the last digit of the serial number. They should join in groups where every other person has that same last number.

Another activity is to ask participants to find someone who, like them, is

- right-handed, left-handed, or ambi-dextrous;
- wearing shoes that tie or shoes without ties;
- an early-morning person or a late-night person;
- wearing rings or not wearing rings;

- a devotee of regular coffee, decaffeinated coffee, or no coffee at all;
- a breakfast-eater or not a breakfast eater;
- a morning-shower person or a night-shower person;
- a Macintosh computer user, an IBM or clone user, a different kind of user, or a non-computer user;
- a summer, fall, winter, or spring baby;
- wearing an item of clothing of a particular color; or
- a shower singer or the silent type.

If you need to move everyone to new tables, provide each person at the table with a slip of paper, each of the same color. (Post-It Notes work well for this.) Use one color per table. To move people to new tables in new groupings, instruct them:

> Make groups of (number), but no two colors should be the same. Your new table groups should have at least one of every color. Say goodbye to your table-mates and find your new ones.

You might decide to use numbers, alphabet letters, animal names, or song titles to re-group people in this fashion. Newspaper cartoons and old calendar pages also work well.

Another method to subdivide a large group involves small squares of construction paper, Post-It Notes, or colored paper clips. Ask people to find all the others in the room with the same color they have and form a group. Assign them an easy, fun topic before getting into the more serious task. For example, "Before you start discussing the question at hand, find the average number of miles you have traveled to this meeting," or "Find the average age of the group" (if that doesn't seem too intrusive; actually, I've seen some people playfully fib about this one).

I once asked a group to find the average number of different jobs represented by the people at their table. This discussion generated lots of interesting conversation and laughter—and this was at a bridal dinner.

The Power of Droodles

Illustrations like those in the book *Classic Droodles* by Roger Price (1992) are one of my favorite meeting tools. As first mentioned in Chapter 4, Droodles are nondescript drawings that can be anything you want them to be. As Price says, "A Droodle doesn't make any sense until you know the correct title" (p. 4). For example, consider the drawing in Figure 7.1.

Some might say that it is a pepperoni pizza, or a petri dish, or a bowling ball for people who like to make decisions! In fact, the picture is whatever your eyes see.

You can prepare Droodles on small sheets of paper and distribute them to meeting participants. (It's fine to draw your own Droo-

Figure 7.1

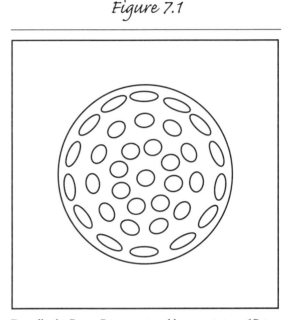

Droodles by Roger Price reprinted by permission of Price Stern Sloan, Inc. from *Classic Droodles*, copyright 1953, © 1981 by Roger Price.

dles. Just draw them. They automatically change with your rendition.) At the appropriate time, ask that participants find all the other people in the room who have the same Droodle as they do (usually about three or four others). When they get together, their task is to figure out what the illustration is. Because there are no right answers, everyone can participate.

This activity always generates lots of laughter and creative thinking. I especially like to use Droodles because they allow me to make the point that we all see things from our own perspectives. And in a meeting of any kind, that's important to remember.

Figure 7.2

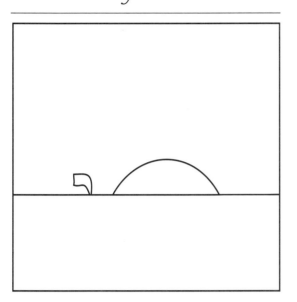

Droodles by Roger Price reprinted by permission of Price Stern Sloan, Inc. from *Classic Droodles*, copyright 1953, © 1981 by Roger Price.

Figure 7.3

Droodles by Roger Price reprinted by permission of Price Stern Sloan, Inc. from *Classic Droodles*, copyright 1953, © 1981 by Roger Price.

After about a minute you can call the group together, show each Droodle on a screen, and invite people to call out what they've decided it is. Droodles are a great conversation stimulator. They invite full participation and creative thinking, and they are always good for a laugh. You might try your hand at producing a few Droodles of your own. Figures 7.2–7.4 are a few more Droodle ideas from *Classic Droodles* (Price, 1992). What do *you* see? In Figure 7.2, is a bald man smoking a pipe? Or is the angle wrong? Is Figure 7.3 a worm taking a date to dinner? And in Figure 7.4, did the bow tie get a little too close to the elevator door?

Creativity Through the Back Door

Another fun way to stimulate people's ideas is the "back-door" approach. For example, you obviously want whatever you're planning to be a great success. One question to brainstorm is: "What are all the ways we can guarantee the *worst* program possible?" In coming up with the answers, people always get a little silly, which then allows them to get serious. For example, "We could make sure that there is no publicity, don't serve any food, don't introduce anyone, set the room temperature very high, and start about an hour late." Once

Figure 7.4

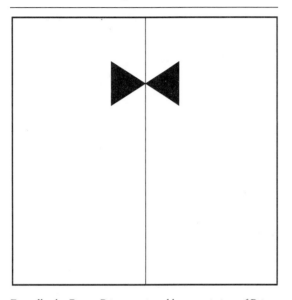

Droodles by Roger Price reprinted by permission of Price Stern Sloan, Inc. from *Classic Droodles*, copyright 1953, © 1981 by Roger Price.

we identify what it takes to make an event fail, it's easy to remember what makes it successful.

When I was a junior high English teacher, I would ask my students, "How would you write a terrible paper?" or "What are some surefire ways we can make certain people will feel uncomfortable in this class?" It's amazing that when people identify how *not* to do something, it leads them to discover how to do it.

Who Goes First?

At certain times in a meeting, training session, or classroom, you have to decide who will go first (or who might win a prize). For example, people are seated at round tables. A question has been posed, and they have to decide who will speak first. You can help by suggesting they start with the person

- whose birthday is closest to today's date;
- whose last two digits of their home phone number are closest to 10 (or whatever number you choose);
- whose hair is the curliest, straightest, or hardest to manage;
- who had the largest (smallest) graduating high school class;
- who has the longest first name;
- who has the shortest last name;
- who most resembles the meeting leader or presenter; or
- whose back is facing the meeting leader or presenter.

Another way to choose someone to begin is to ask everyone to put their index finger in the air. Then say, "At the count of three, point to the person at your table who should start. That person can accept or, instead, *choose* the person to begin." This process can be used to select a group leader or recorder.

☺   ☺   ☺

When we ask people to make choices about whom to sit with, whom to work with, and who should speak first, we create tension, however minor. To build group camaraderie, provide tasks in which everyone can participate equally, such as determining what a Droodle might be or switching to a new table according to the color of a Post-It Note. A light-hearted approach like this reduces tension and moves participants into new groups with ease, setting the stage for a more productive meeting.

8

Fun with Food

If you're looking for an easy way to bring levity to your next meeting, search no farther than the refreshment table. One of the easiest ways to lighten up your gathering is to serve something different from the usual coffee, doughnuts, and bagels.

At Hayes Elementary School, staff meetings often begin at the end of the school day and stretch into the dinner hour. The principal and 12 teachers share the task of bringing refreshments. Everyone looks forward to Ann Roberts's turn because she always comes up with something fun and different. Is this because she teaches kindergarten and can still think like a 5-year-old? Whereas others resort to a conventional bag of pretzels or cookies, Ann has been known to provide all-day suckers or cupcakes decorated with clown faces.

Comfort Food

A surefire way to lighten the mood of your meetings is with snacks that harken back to childhood. Of course you'll want to offer healthy food such as yogurt, fresh or dried fruit, low-fat baked goods, or granola. But how about adding lollipops, Tootsie Rolls, ice cream cones, sweetened cereal, popcorn, Jello Jigglers, candy hearts, decorated cupcakes, or dot candies on paper strips to your next refreshment table?

In a parenting class, each person brought a favorite childhood food: Spaghettios, peanut butter and jelly sandwiches, peanut butter and mustard sandwiches, chicken noodle soup, chocolate chip cookies, and Twinkies. Can you imagine going into a professional meeting and seeing a bunch of candy waxed lips lying on the refreshment table?

We associate food with comfort, and refreshments in general set an inviting tone. Food turns the mood of the meeting into something more homelike. Fun foods also trigger memories and get people talking and laughing together. We associate fun foods with parties and celebrations. Food is a means of connecting people and creating comfort and a relaxed atmosphere.

Not only the food itself but the *way* it is served can invite smiles. I was the afternoon speaker at an all-day professional development retreat for about 50 management staff members. Lunch was provided buffet style. As people were finishing their meals and still sitting at their tables, I playfully took a platter of wonderfully large, tasty cookies around to each person and offered them as dessert. People were surprised and appreciative. I laughed, too, because it's really fun to serve other people's cookies. And the very act of serving the cookies gave me an opportunity to introduce myself and establish rapport right away. The group that eats, plays, and laughs together will more likely pay attention in the meeting.

The Power of the Prune

You can serve food that not only tastes good and is good for you, but you also can serve snacks that tickle the funny bone. Prunes do that! There is something amusing about those little wrinkled fruits: They look funny, they sound funny, and they do funny things to us. Even when you say the word, your face does something funny: It puckers.

At a training event, the meeting planner produced a lovely array of fruits, muffins, bagels, juices, and yogurts, along with a beautiful glass bowl filled with something few recognized. It was a bowl of prunes. Unfortunately, they had all stuck together, but they still had

the desired effect. When people found out what they were, they laughed heartily.

Serving something funny catches people off guard and gives them something silly to talk about. It's not threatening, and it doesn't take away from the seriousness of the meeting. In fact, *because* the meeting is serious, it's important to plan for laughter so that things don't become too solemn. Sharing fun foods helps everyone to stay on the lighter side and relax.

Non-Food Funniness

In addition to the food and beverages, consider the serving utensils and paper goods. At a large association luncheon meeting, the planners invited a bit of laughter by using Bugs Bunny napkins along with the beautiful table service provided by the hotel. In addition, to speed up the luncheon so that the speaker would have plenty of time for her presentation, dessert was put on the tables at the beginning of the meal: large yellow happy-face cookies for everyone. Later in the afternoon, a more substantial dessert of fruit and popcorn was served.

Mealtime Conversation

Have you ever been seated at a table during a meal break where you knew no one and sensed you had nothing in common with your table partners? You know the drill. You introduce yourself to the person on your right and try to strike up a conversation. But it drifts.

The salad is served. Suddenly you notice the person to your right is chatting with the person on his right. The two people on your left are actively engaged, as well. You feel a little excluded, so you concentrate on buttering your roll and hope the main course comes soon. You wish you'd chosen another table.

Shy people will recognize this scenario. So will the not-so-shy who find themselves sitting next to someone who turns out to be truly boring because all she does is talk about herself. As the meeting planner or leader, you'd like to spare everyone this kind of discomfort. One solution is "The Secret Envelope." Though this activity can be adapted for several places in the meeting, it works especially well at a meal.

There is something magical about a sealed package, whether it's a box as big as the doorway or a slender sealed envelope. What surprises does it hold? To create a Secret Envelope, first prepare eight small slips of paper (or one for every person at the table) with one question on each slip. Number the papers one through eight, starting with the question that requires the least amount of thinking and moving to those that require a little more brainwork. The questions can be personal (though not too personal), or they can be related to the theme of the meeting and issues you wish to be raised. (See Appendix A for a variety of questions to stimulate conversations.)

Now put the eight slips of paper into an envelope, and label it "Secret Envelope." You can decorate the envelope if you like, but it's not necessary. Place the envelope in the center of the table with the directions from Figure 8.1. (These should be written on a separate sheet of paper, folded, and attached to the outside of the envelope.)

The directions in Figure 8.1 ask the person with the curliest hair to open the envelope. Other ways to determine who should open the envelope could be as follows: the person with a birthday closest to _____ (pick a date—maybe your own birthday); the person with the most letters in his or her first name or last name; or the person who traveled the most miles to be at the meeting. Any category that applies to everyone at the table will work.

Here are a few categories that may help you select appropriate questions for your group. The first questions are more conventional and less likely to generate an interesting or laugh-evoking discussion; but everyone has an answer, and the questions require little thinking and help people connect with one another right away. However, be sure to include at least one question from each category to ensure variety and meaning in the conversations.

- *Easy-to-answer, generic conversation starters such as:* Where were you born? Where did you grow up? Where else have you lived? What's the name of the street you lived at the longest? Which childhood telephone number(s) do you remember?

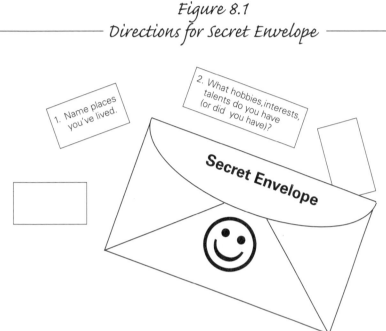

Figure 8.1
Directions for Secret Envelope

1. Name places you've lived.

2. What hobbies, interests, talents do you have (or did you have)?

Secret Envelope

Directions:

1. The person with the curliest hair takes the envelope and opens it.

2. Distribute questions to each person at the table, one per person. If there are fewer than eight people, give some people two questions.

3. The person with Question 1: Read the question aloud. Answer it. All the other people at the table also answer the question, although they may pass if they wish.

4. Person with Question 2: Read the question aloud. Again, each person responds—and on and on through Question 8.

5. **The purpose of this is to stimulate interesting, fun conversation.** Don't worry if you don't make it through all of the questions, although knowing what possibilities for discovery lie in the answers, I encourage you to do so! **Have a good time!**

• *Memory-evoking questions guaranteed to bring about humorous remarks and laughter, such as:* As a child, what do you remember wanting to be when you grew up? And now what are you doing? What Saturday morning or after-school cartoons do you remember watching? What radio shows did you listen to? What clothing fads were popular when you were in high school? What do you remember about your first day on the job?

• *Just for laughs questions, such as:* If we were to visit you at home or work, what's something amusing you'd probably want us to see? What *wouldn't* you want us to see? (maybe your garage or under your bed). What are some memories you have about coloring with crayons? What were some of your favorite childhood candies? What's one of the most humorous gifts you can remember either receiving or giving?

• *Fun and games questions, such as:* What do you do for fun? What childhood games do you remember playing? What toys did you play with? What toys did you "create"? At work, what kinds of things make it fun? Who can you count on to make you laugh?

• *Questions that help people get to know one another on a deeper level, such as:* What positive "first" did you experience this past year, either personally or professionally? If you

Figure 8.2

Reprinted by permission of Ashleigh Brilliant. Copyright © 1985 by Ashleigh Brilliant.

could have a conversation with a famous person, whom would you choose? And what would you want to talk about? What special hobbies, interests, or talents do you have? If you could be an assistant to someone, whom would you choose? Why? What's something you want to learn or do before you leave this earth? What do you usually do on Sundays? What's your favorite magazine, and why? What's something you hate to do? What is one of your most prized material possessions? Where is a place you feel really comfortable? If your name has a story, tell us about it. How did you get your first name? What is one idea you've picked up so far today that's made this worth the price of admission?

☺   ☺   ☺

Although it is not always a necessary ingredient of your meeting, food—and stimulating mealtime conversation—plays no small role in re-energizing participants and creating opportunities for a positive meeting experience. Perhaps another of Ashleigh Brilliant's Pot Shots (Figure 8.2) best sums up the importance of fun food in meetings.

Breaks That Invigorate

All meeting planners would do well to remember the adage, "The mind can absorb what the seat can endure."

Most of us can stay on task only for a certain period before we get restless. If your meeting is going to run longer than 90 minutes, you probably need to plan for a break. That allows people to clear their minds, take care of physical needs, and attend to personal matters. A break also provides another opportunity to add a little levity to keep the meeting moving toward its goal.

You want participants to come back from their break refreshed and eager to begin again with renewed purpose. Keep in mind, however, that there's no such thing as a five-minute break. How often have you been disappointed when you allot five minutes for a break, but people don't come back on time? That's because it usually takes longer than five minutes to take care of personal matters. Ten minutes

should be the minimum for a break; 15 is even better.

Send Them Out—and Lure Them Back—with a Smile

To get more "smileage" out of your break, announce it with a short, funny video or a humorous slide or transparency. You also might consider playing lively music to signal the start of the break. You can play this same music to call attendees back to the meeting, or you can gather them with a silly horn or a bell.

One meeting leader playfully threatens that everyone must be seated by the time the music ends or they will have to do something funny in front of the group. He prepares lighthearted, safe gags ahead of time, such as reciting a nursery rhyme or singing a silly, familiar song. Participants sometimes come up with their own bits as well.

Before you send participants on a break, pique their interest in what's going to happen afterwards by telling them what to expect when they return. For example, you can get them back smiling by telling them there will be a drawing for a prize when they return. To be eligible, they must be seated on time. Or simply announce that there will be a surprise waiting for them when they return to their seats. You might be amazed at how motivating this can be, or how much people enjoy finding simple surprises like childhood candies, trinkets, or old cartoon calendar pages at their places.

Beginning Again

When you restart the meeting, you'll want people to mentally return to the matters at hand. But this may take a bit of refocusing. Show a snappy quote or cartoon on the screen. Consider providing a puzzle or brain-teaser that draws people's attention away from the activities during the break and back to the business of the meeting. Read or tell a humorous story or anecdote. One of my favorites is a "letter" from a college student to her parents, shown in Figure 9.1.

There are many variations of this letter, and this one is courtesy of "jollytologist" Allen Klein, author of *The Healing Power of Humor* (1989, pp. 13–14). I often use the letter to make the point that our sense of humor works like magic, helping us to turn things around. Our sense of humor helps

Figure 9.1
A "Letter" from College

Dear Mom and Dad,

I am sorry that I have not written, but all my stationery was destroyed when the dorm burned down. I am now out of the hospital, and the doctor said that I will be fully recovered soon. I have also moved in with the boy who rescued me, since most of my things were destroyed in the fire.

Oh yes, I know that you have always wanted a grandchild, so you will be pleased to know that I am pregnant and you will have one soon.

Love,

Mary

P.S. There was no fire, my health is perfectly fine, and I am not pregnant. In fact, I do not even have a boyfriend. However, I did get a D in French and a C in math and chemistry, and I just wanted to make sure that you keep it all in perspective.

Source: The Healing Power of Humor by Allen Klein, 1989, Los Angeles: Jeremy Tarcher. Adapted by permission

us feel more positive—even about negative facts. Using the letter or another anecdote sets the stage for returning to the substance of the meeting with a constructive frame of mind.

Picking Grapes

You also might refocus attention by leading participants in a simple physical energizer. My favorite is "Picking Grapes," which I learned from the folks at The Humor Project in Saratoga Springs, New York. The directions go something like this:

• Ask everyone to stand up (or they can remain seated if they prefer).

• Then tell them, "Imagine that above you is a bunch of grapes. There are lots of bunches of grapes, and they are perfect for plucking right now. In fact, if they aren't harvested soon, they'll just fall down to the ground and go to waste. With your right hand high above you, reach for some grapes, pick them, and place them in your left hand. See how many you can collect in 15 seconds. Be careful not to drop them!"

• You should get involved with this playfully, too. For example, reach high, calling out words of encouragement like, "Reach, reach, reach! Oh, I see some more right there!"

• Now, ask participants to carefully set their grapes on the ground in front of them. They should then move a little away from the grapes and reach with the left hand for more grapes.

• Instruct them, "There are still a lot more to be plucked! Put them into your right hand . . . reach and pluck, reach and pluck, reach, reach, reach!" The pickers should be careful not to step on the grapes behind them or next to them. This can take 15 seconds more.

• Now instruct everyone, "Carefully put these grapes in the pile with your others. Admire your collection. You have so many! Of course, what do we make from grapes? [wine or juice] So what do we do with those grapes on the ground? We stomp on them! So, stomp, stomp, stomp!" At this point, spend about 10 seconds in vigorous stomping!

The energy that this one-minute activity generates is wonderful. There's always laughter at the silliness; and, more important, everyone's bodies are invigorated. Then they are ready to resume the meeting tasks. I like the activity, too, because it can be done either sitting or standing, which includes everyone in the group. For additional delightful ways to recharge through physical fun, see the book *Playfair* (Weinstein & Goodman, 1980).

☺   ☺   ☺

However you decide to structure the time, a break is another chance to invite humor into your meeting without taking away from the serious business. Thoughtfully consider what you might do before, during, or after a break. Sometimes you'll want to plan for purposeful fun; other times, you'll just want to break the routine. Whatever your choice, seek to make the most out of your breaks, as you do with the rest of the agenda.

10

Ending the Meeting
on a Positive Note

"Are there any questions or comments?" How many times have you asked this at the end of a meeting, only to be met with silence?

It's natural to assume that when no one raises a hand to ask a question or offer a comment, the participants really don't have anything more to say. But in reality, most people choose to remain silent in a group because they are uncomfortable with speaking up. Or sometimes it's because of time pressures (they just want to get out of there!) Or maybe it's because they're shy about asking what they think is a "dumb" question.

Isn't it curious, though, that we become very chatty right after a meeting adjourns? How often have you stood in the hallway, parking lot, or stairwell following a meeting, suddenly finding yourself full of ideas for the group and wondering why you didn't think of them earlier? Many times, some of the very best ideas, conversations, and decisions emerge *after* a meeting ends. Maybe our meetings should start with the adjournment! At the very least we should consider putting Steven Covey's advice into practice: "Begin with the end in mind" (1989, p. 97).

In all seriousness, think about the conclusion of your meeting, gathering, or special event.

☺   Beginning with the ending in mind, what do you want to have accomplished?

☺   How do you want people to feel as they leave?

☺   If they tell others about the meeting, what do you hope they will say? How would you like them to describe what went on?

My desired outcome is always that we got the work done *and* we had some fun. I want meetings to have enjoyable, satisfying aspects even if the work is tough or a difficult decision must be made.

Ask for Positive Comments

To conclude on a positive note, ask participants to reflect on the good things about the
meeting. Perhaps it's the work that was accomplished, the mood or tone of the meeting,
the insights, or the expectations for the future. A useful question to pose is "What one
fact, idea, or insight was raised or learned?"

Sometimes you can end a meeting with a
conversation starter like, "When you leave
here and get back home or to work, someone
might ask what you did at this meeting. What
are you going to tell them that was positive?"
Depending on the size of the group, I may ask
participants to talk in pairs before sharing
their answers with the whole gathering. In
fact, whenever you want to increase participation in discussions, give people a chance to
talk about an idea with another person before
they share it with everyone else. It's more reassuring for participants to test a comment with
someone else before stating it aloud.

Another approach is to hang a large sheet
of paper in a convenient spot. Then invite
people to write down positive memories of
the meeting (or event, or school year, or whatever you want their feedback on). Participants might want to talk about their words or
pictures before the whole group, or they may
just want to put them to paper with no comment at all.

The bimonthly seminars of the Professional Speakers Association of Michigan end
with participants discussing, and then writing

on Post-It Notes, some of their ideas, observations, and points of interest. The notes are
then placed on a large sheet of paper and
printed in the next edition of the newsletter.
This process serves several purposes: It gets
people talking about what went on, it provides a group summary, and each person is invited to participate in the feedback portion of
the meeting.

For special end-of-year meetings, you
might consider generating feedback through
the following questions. For example, ask students or staff members to give advice to pro-
spective students or staff: "If you were trying
to convince someone you know to be a student or a staff member in our school, what
would you tell him or her about it?" This question can be rephrased for any group.

To help meeting participants reflect on
their own growth, pose sentence starters that
emphasize the positive:

• In the past (day, week, month, year),
I've learned that I . . .
• Before I started school this year I didn't
(or couldn't) . . . but now I can (or know how
to, or know) . . .
• I am happy that I . . .
• I was surprised to learn that I . . .
• I always used to . . . but now I . . .

Be sure to remind people of the meaningful work they have done, whether it was making decisions, networking with others,
teaching and learning, celebrating, or all of

the above. Participants will leave on an upbeat note if they summarize the positives and provide encouragement for continued successes. Sometimes it's appropriate to ask people to find a buddy whom they will call to report progress during the week.

Evaluation Forms

When we ask people to evaluate the meeting, it's important to remember to actually use the information for future planning. On more than one occasion, I've asked for feedback and then forgotten to make use of it when preparing the next meeting. Does that sound familiar to you?

Evaluation forms themselves can evoke smiles. Figure 10.1 (see p. 78) is one form I like to use after a presentation.

If you're a little daring, you might try the evaluation question posed by Ashleigh Brilliant in Figure 10.2 (see p. 79).

Saying Good-Bye

For a physical, silly way to say good-bye to people, try the "wiggle handshake" (Weinstein & Goodman, 1980). There are three steps to this handshake. First you shake a person's hand. Then you clasp thumbs. Then, with your thumbs still clasped, you open your hand and wave your fingers. It's fun to do and to watch, sort of like a secret handshake. If it's used in an ongoing team or other group, it can become "our special greeting."

Sometimes I ask people to stand up, put their hands out in front of them, clap them together slowly, then increase the pace and break the rhythm. Before you know it, you have a standing ovation!

It also can be helpful to conclude with a fun token of appreciation. Provide a little gift for everyone to take along, a little piece of silliness, perhaps, or something just for fun: a magic wand, a balloon, a crown. One of my favorite gifts is a small "Happy Rock®." Art teacher Carol C. Steele produces the little painted happy-face rocks and distributes them with these directions:

> Give a HAPPY ROCK to someone you love. Watch them smile! Slowly but surely, the smile of the giver will fade from the Happy Rock as it is absorbed into the heart of the receiver. Not for human consumption. DO NOT EAT. Product is made of glass. Not intended for children under 5.

(For ordering Happy Rocks and other resources, see "Spirit Lifters" in the Resources section.)

If you want to make people feel especially good, end your meeting a little bit earlier than scheduled!

Summarizing the Meeting

In their classic book *How to Make Meetings Work*, Doyle and Straus (1993) make the case for using a Group Memory. This is an effec-

Figure 10.1

— *Evaluation and Reflection Form* —

Please mark the squares that are appropriate for you.

I would ❑ definitely ❑ maybe ❑ definitely not
encourage some people I know to take part in a program like this one.

(Please specify the types of people you have in mind.)

❑ **WOW!** I learned something brand new today! (If possible, please indicate what it was.}

❑ **AHA!** I had a flash of insight--a new understanding--a "So THAT explains it" kind of sensation.

❑ **AHH. . .** I never thought of it like that before! I got a new way of thinking about something I've known for some time.

❑ **HA HA HA . . .** I laughed a lot. THAT sure felt GOOD!

❑ **UH HUH! YUP!** I found myself agreeing with the things that were said. It's a good feeling to know that the speaker and I are on the same wavelength

One thing I want to try really soon is . . .

About your presentation, I want to say . . .

❑ And you can use my name as a reference if you want to. Here it is, along with my title and phone number. I'd be happy to have you contact me for further thoughts.

Figure 10.2

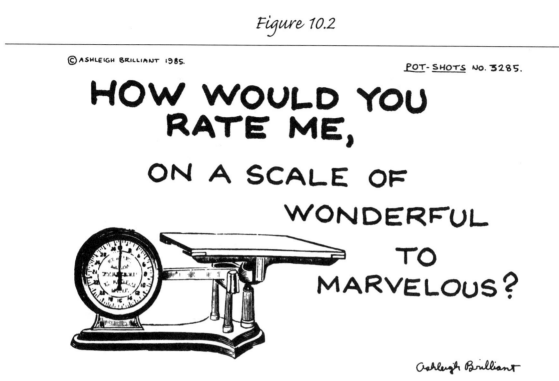

Reprinted by permission of Ashleigh Brilliant. Copyright © 1985 by Ashleigh Brilliant.

tive way to involve all participants in recording what happened. As discussions take place, a group member records suggestions and observations on flipchart paper that can be seen by all. Because the items are visible to everyone, they are more accurately recorded. Depending on the kind of room and equipment you have, computers or overhead projectors might also be used for recording everyone's contributions.

This kind of recording, followed by summarizing, is a great opportunity for adding a little levity at the end of a meeting. You also can ask each person to write down several things on Post-It Notes, read them aloud, and then place them on chart paper. Supply humorous Post-Its for an added chuckle.

As with other printed matter, you can add some lighthearted artwork to your minutes or summary when you send it out. You might include an announcement like this in your next minutes: "At our next meeting, Joan will bring jellybeans, and John will supply some funny cartoons. Please bring your smiles along."

☺ ☺ ☺

To keep his summaries lighthearted and inviting, one humorous fund-raising chairman ends with, "Milk and cookies were served. A good time was had by all." With a closing like that, who wouldn't look forward to the beginning of the next meeting?

11

The Power of saying Thanks

In our busy lives, it's easy to overlook common courtesies. One of these is the simple thank-you note. Although we don't have any control over others' behavior, we certainly control our own. Sending a note of thanks is just good manners, and it's an opportunity to invite a smile at the same time. Whether participation in meetings is voluntary or demanded by our job, it is always rewarding and motivating to send—and receive—a note of appreciation.

Thank-You Notes

One of the most original thank-you's I've ever seen was given by a woman I met at a National Speakers Association meeting. By chance, we were sitting at the same table, having a cup of coffee. As people do at networking meetings, we began to talk. Our conversation was both delightful and interesting.

Of greater fascination, however, was the note I found later on the floor in my hotel room (see Figure 11.1, on the next page). Clearly, it had been slipped under the door so that I would see it when I came in.

Figure 11.2 (on p. 82) shows another thank-you from a member of a committee I had chaired for a special conference. This note was just one of several responses to the brief thank-you card and small gift that I had given as a token of my appreciation to each of 10 steering-committee members.

You can be sure that I was as excited to give the gifts as the planning group was to receive them. But the delightful "thank you for the thank-you note" took me by complete surprise. And I must confess, it made me feel very good. Do you think I'd like to work with this committee again? You bet. They were eager, dependable, and appreciative of each other's contributions. Equally important, we

Figure 11.1

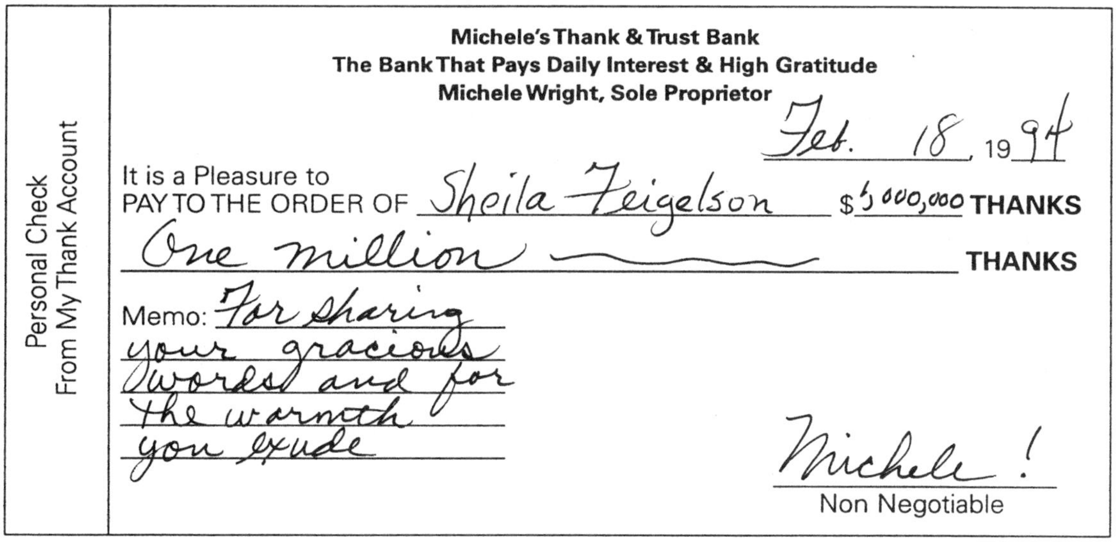

> **Michele's Thank & Trust Bank**
> **The Bank That Pays Daily Interest & High Gratitude**
> **Michele Wright, Sole Proprietor**
>
> *Feb. 18*, 19*94*
>
> It is a Pleasure to
> PAY TO THE ORDER OF *Sheila Feigelson* $*5,000,000* **THANKS**
>
> *One million* ———————— **THANKS**
>
> Memo: *For sharing your gracious words and for the warmth you exude*
>
> *Michele !*
> ————————
> Non Negotiable

Personal Check / From My Thank Account

Note: Adapted by permission of Michele Wright.

could count on some good laughs as we planned the event. Maybe that's why we were all so eager, dependable, and appreciative. Our meetings were brightened by laughter.

Consider the card of appreciation sent by a colleague after I facilitated the participant introductions at our bimonthly association meeting. On one side was a photo of her running in a marathon; the printed caption reads: "Unless you move—where you are is where you will always be." On the flip side, her handwritten message said, "Your warm-up was terrific. Thanks for the idea. Cindy Jones." How do you think I felt when I received this note?

If you're saying wonderful, appreciated, and happy—you're right!

From the president of an organization I belong to came this appreciative note:

> Thanks so much for serving on the Nominating Committee this year. The new board is terrific and we are all looking forward to a wonderful year together. Your efforts are greatly appreciated. Thanks for all that you do.

Although this note isn't humorous, it was most definitely heartfelt. And I knew it. Because my efforts were appreciated, you can be

Figure 11.2
—— *Thanks for the Thank You!* ——

Dear Sheila,

Thanks so much for your lovely note and the "Happy Rocks." It was very kind of you to do this for me. I always admire the "special touch" you give to people and events. I look forward to many more opportunities of getting together! You did a fabulous job!

Love,

Ester

sure that I'd be willing to work with them again.

Balloons and Things

You don't always have to write out a thank you. At a weekly staff meeting, the director arrived with a bouquet of helium-filled Mylar balloons, the long-lasting kind. The colors were vibrant, and the sight of them brought to mind a circus or carnival. When someone asked what they were for, the director replied, "I just hoped they would cheer you up. You've

been working very hard, and I appreciate it so much. Each of you take one back to your desk when we're done." The balloons brightened the office for days and reminded everyone that there is always room for fun at work.

I once facilitated a school staff workshop about managing change. Keeping a sense of humor is an important part of dealing with the rapid rate of change in our lives. We talked about the power of humor and laughter for coping with the stress that often accompanies change. The program had gone well, and I was pleased with the group's response. A week later, I was pleased again when I received the note in Figure 11.3 from one of the group members. The paper it was written on obviously came from a calendar.

Chiropractor and professional speaker Jenna Eisenberg has a delightful way of showing people she cares about them, whether they are current or future clients. She sends them a postcard. One side shows a baby picture of herself, holding and squeezing her favorite doll. The caption says, "Dr. Jenna Eisenberg, chiropractor and speaker, giving her first adjustment at age 9 months. She began speaking shortly after." On the other side is printed:

> Jenna's Idea of the Week: Carry Your Baby Picture With You! Show others who can't see how cute you still are—how cute you still are. (Remind yourself too!) You can create

Figure 11.3
——— *A Special Note* ———

> **February 19**
>
> *Dear Sheila,*
>
> *When I opened my book of daily contemplations last night, this was the passage for the day. How appropriate and true. I thought you would enjoy having this. Thanks again. It was useful, insightful, and most of all, fun.*
>
> *Sincerely,*
>
> *Lucy*
>
> ---
> In pure laughter you get in touch with your own love, your own joy. And it is this pure laughter, laughter with complete freedom, that beautifies God's creation. This is what really brings greatness into one's life. When people laugh from the heart, you experience God in their laughter.
>
> —Swami Chidvilasananda

more laughter and stronger fun connections with people around you.

P.S. You can use my picture if you don't have one of your own! Call for a treatment or to book a speaking date. This baby loves her work!

A friendly reminder, a note of thanks, or a simple gesture of appreciation goes a long way toward motivating people to attend and participate in meetings. Humorous cards, small trinkets, and sincerely expressed words of appreciation help keep people's spirits up and hopeful. In the words attributed to film producer Samuel Goldwyn, "When someone does something good, applaud! Then you will make two people happy" (Klein, 1991, p. 67).

12

Inviting Laughter to Your Next Meeting

It's been said that when people are smiling, they are receptive to almost anything you teach them. Common sense tells us that people are more ready to listen and learn when they're in a positive frame of mind. Shared laughter helps to create that mindset.

In this book, we've looked at four major topics:

☺ **Why** humor is so important in meetings, gatherings, and special events.

☺ **When** humor can be appropriately and effectively used before, during, and after a meeting.

☺ **What** to consider when choosing your humor. Criteria include: Does your choice help or hinder the goals of your meeting? Is the humor constructive or destructive?

☺ **How** to invite laughter into your serious—and not so serious—meetings and still be productive.

This chapter will take one last look at the power and importance of humor in meetings.

The ETC Principle

The power of humor is an intriguing subject. The word itself seems to defy any one agreed-upon definition. Mel Helitzer, teacher of comedy writing and funny thinking, notes, "In matters of humor, what is appealing to one person may be appalling to another" (cited in Wilson, 1990, p. 137).

As a workshop leader and speaker, I've explored the benefits and liabilities of humor with a lot of groups. Eventually, I created "The ETC Principle," a simple mnemonic device to summarize the impact of humor on meetings, organizations, relationships, and daily life.

• Humor **E**nlivens, **E**ncourages, **E**ntertains, **E**nriches, **E**nlightens.

- Humor Tickles, Touches, Teaches, relieves Tension, Turns Things around.
- Humor Communicates, Creates bonds between people, helps Cope with stress.

Along the way, I've also found a few liabilities of humor, which are also encompassed by The ETC Principle.

- When used inappropriately, humor can Embarrass and Enrage someone.
- Humor can create Tension, and sometimes Transform a positive into a negative.
- Humor Can Cause Confusion. ("Can't you take a joke?")

Keep all of these aspects in mind when considering whether your choice of a fun, lighthearted approach will be viewed as helpful or harmful; amusing or abusing; moving the meeting forward or taking it off-track.

From Sad to Glad

On the morning of January 14, 1991, there was tremendous tension in the world, the United States, and my house. Following Iraq's invasion of Kuwait, the threat of war in the Persian Gulf was becoming very real. A deadline for withdrawal of Iraqi troops had been set, but Iraq's leader was defying ultimatums. All of us were glued to the TV. The consequences of any actions taken by the United States seemed ominous. I felt as if things were totally out of control. To see our leaders so disheartened was terribly demoralizing. As a par-

ent and as a citizen, I was nearly immobilized with fear and concern.

I had been scheduled to meet with a University of Michigan administrator later in the day to plan a humor workshop for a group of residence hall counselors. Suddenly it seemed so trivial, so unimportant. I considered canceling, but in the end I kept our appointment.

I came into the administrator's office feeling down, and we talked about the world situation for nearly half an hour. I knew that we had to get to the major point of our meeting, but it was difficult to leave the heavy emotion of the world.

Finally, we began talking about the workshop. As I described what I do to help people lighten up, I found that I began to lighten up myself. Just *talking* about humor helped us both feel better. And I was reminded once again of how we can bring forth laughter just by talking about funny topics. Powerful stuff! It felt good for a moment be away from the worries of the world.

Life *is* serious. There is always the threat of something bad or dangerous happening, even if it is not on the scale of war. We can't control world events, but we can soothe ourselves through laughter and keep our sanity.

Laughing Matters for Serious Meetings

By now, you know that I've planned many meetings and go to considerable lengths to bring humor to them in productive and helpful ways. What follows are two examples of meetings I've planned. My hope is that sharing the planning process may help you see how to weigh many of the factors and considerations in planning for humor. We don't have to leave laughter to chance; we can purposely invite it along. As you read these examples, think about how they illustrate the use of humor and fun to meet different purposes, using many of the ideas presented in the pages of this book. And keep in mind the advice of author Allen Klein (1989): "A bit of pre-planned humor . . . is like having a psychological insurance policy: You may never need it, but it sure is nice to know it's there if you do" (p. 46).

The Accountants' Retreat

I was invited to facilitate a daylong retreat for the seven partners of a successful accounting firm. The business had prospered for 25 years, and the partners, all men aged 32–71, enjoyed good working relationships. Two of the founding partners were preparing to retire in the next five years. They needed to make plans for how the firm would continue to grow and prosper. There was some tension around this, of course, as there always is when planning for the unknown.

Two weeks before the meeting, I interviewed each of the seven partners to learn what kinds of issues were on their minds and what they wanted to have happen as a result of the retreat. At the end of each interview, I gave the person a "magic wand"—a tube

filled with fluid and floating glitter. This was just a little lighthearted way to set a tone for something magical to happen at their retreat. I was purposely planting the idea that even though the day's work was serious, it didn't have to be solemn. And in fact, something magical could come of it—as indeed it did.

When I sat down to plan the day, I consciously thought about ways to lighten the serious agenda and at the same time stay focused on the major goal: to make decisions about the future of the firm. Were I to classify this type of meeting, I would certainly call it a *decision-making* meeting, though elements of each of the four major meeting types discussed in Chapter 2 were apparent. The partners would *network* (get better acquainted with each other), *learn* (review the history of the firm and things that were affecting the future direction), and *celebrate* (eat together, have special snacks, let each other know how they appreciate one another). Still, we knew that the overall goal was to make decisions.

My choices of "humor injection" were affected by that goal. Whatever we did, I wanted to create a climate where people could be honest about their concerns, express their appreciation of what was good, and feel safe in raising issues. I needed them to trust me and each other.

I knew that as part of their planning process at the retreat, the men would identify all kinds of preferred images of the future, listing them on flipchart paper. At some point, they would have to prioritize the items, which would require some type of voting. To indicate their vote, I gave each person a sheet of little round yellow stickers with "happy face" symbols. Each person was allowed five votes. They were to peel off the sticker and place it next to each of the five items of their choice. Just seeing the newsprint sheets dotted with smiley-face stickers gave the activity a sense of playfulness. It cast their preferred image of the future in a positive light.

At another point in the meeting, each person had a chance to tell the others some things about himself. They shared such things as

- memories of what it was like when they first joined the firm;
- what they were proud of;
- something they considered a personal success;
- something they considered a professional success;
- a success of the past week;
- what they anticipated for the next few weeks; and
- an area in which they wanted to get some help.

They took turns, one at a time. After each person was finished speaking, the others were to give a genuine compliment to him, telling what they saw as the person's strengths and what they appreciated about him. To make this part meaningful, memorable, and visible, each person was given a sheet of paper ($8\frac{1}{2}$" x 11") with a bull's-eye on it. The others were to write their compliments on a gummed label, say the compliment out loud, and place it on the bull's eye.

In exercises of this sort, trainers usually use plain white gummed labels, the kind you just peel off and stick on. As I was shopping for supplies for this particular meeting, I found some bright, multicolored labels, six on a sheet. At the meeting, I gave each person three sheets of labels, saying they could write something on as many as three or as few as one; it all depended on the size of their handwriting.

It was amazing to see how lively and colorful the table became with these sheets of colored stickers spread out at each person's place. I realized that we can add lightness to a meeting just by providing some colorful papers and stickers. They were positively cheery, and of course, I commented on that! The partners agreed. And they joked about it, which helped to reduce the tension around the activity of giving compliments.

One of the partners kiddingly remarked, "I wrote my comments on the green sticker for you since I know that money is your favorite color!"

Another said, "I used gold for you since I know you're color blind and it really doesn't matter which color I use, anyhow!"

The serious work of the retreat day was punctuated with laughter and good feelings. Most of it was spontaneous, but I planted the seeds for the good humor with no more than a magic wand, a few happy-face stickers, and colorful adhesive labels.

A Meeting of School Administrators

I had been invited to do a workshop on "Energizing Meetings" for a group of "meet-inged-out" school administrators. For many of them, their long days consist of going from one meeting to another, some of which are useful, others of which are boring and a seeming waste of time.

In my mind, this meeting was primarily a *learning* event for these hard-working, stressed-out leaders. They were eager to discover ways to lighten up on themselves and bring a little more levity to their own staff meetings. In addition, this was a *networking* meeting. The 25 participants knew each other (at least by name and job title), but they didn't necessarily have many opportunities to share ideas with one another in a meeting setting. The meeting was also a *celebration* of sorts. The professional development office included a nice dinner as part of the program to show appreciation for the hard work these leaders do.

Well before the event, I met with Karen Schulte, the facilitator who was in charge. Together we came up with some things to make this meeting special. For example, the staff-development coordinator sent a light-hearted, appealing invitation to each administrator (see sample in Chapter 2).

As people arrived at the 5:00 p.m. meeting, they were instructed to sit at a table that was reserved for them. A different "reserved for" sign was at each table. Participants could select their place from the following:

- This table is reserved for people who know the words to the "Brady Bunch" theme song.
- This table is reserved for people who were out of the country this past year.
- This table is reserved for people who know how to hum or sing two commercials.
- This table is reserved for people who experienced a professional or personal positive first this past year.
- This table is reserved for people who know a quote.
- This table is reserved for people who can recite the alphabet backwards.

On each table were blank nametags. Individuals created a badge by including name, place of birth, and one number of special significance. In addition, on each table there were small baskets of assorted candies, including lollipops, corn candies, chocolate kisses, and dot-candies on paper strips.

Participants were directed to get their dinner from the buffet table. To invite a chuckle, dessert consisted of smiley-face cookie, along with fresh fruit.

As people finished eating, I supplied each of them with a Human Treasure Hunt titled "Gee, I didn't know that . . . " (see sample in Appendix B). Their task was to complete as many items as they could before the group was called together.

At 6:15, Karen officially welcomed everyone and introduced me. I began by announcing that the purpose of the evening's meeting was to explore some ways to energize meetings. To begin, I wanted to know if anyone needed help completing their Human Treasure Hunt. Sure enough, someone said, "I can't find anyone born in my birthday month, October."

I asked, "Is there someone else born then?" There was one other person. I continued by saying, "We know that in a group of about 25 people, there is a pretty good chance that two people will have the exact same birthday. Not necessarily the same year, but the date. Let's do a little research to find out how many pairs this group has. What's your guess? One? Two? Three? None? More? Will someone please keep track of how many pairs we have. Also, keep track of which is the most popular month. What's your guess about which month has the most births? Also, keep track of which number seems to recur most often."

With audience interest heightened, I began our "research."

"All those born in October, please stand up." And they did. I suggested, "Call out your birth date," and received the answers 12, 3, 13, and 12. Great cheers erupted when we discovered that there was already one pair! I provided a small prize for the birthday mates. (It was my "Free Ticket"—see Chapter 5.) Then I directed them, "As long as you're standing, tell us what you wrote on your nametag: where you were born, your number and why it's significant."

We continued on through the months of the year. Interest stayed high. All participants had a chance to say their birth date and then to share a little information about themselves that they had already considered as they prepared their nametags. It was intriguing for all as they learned new things about one another. And they paid attention because they were listening for similarities of birthdates and other information. They made comments like "I didn't know that about you! I was born in Minnesota, too!" Or "That's my sister's birthday!"

We went on to other unanswered Treasure Hunt questions, and the administrators talked about how they could modify the activity to suit their own staff.

The rest of the evening focused on the parts of every meeting that lend themselves to a little levity without diminishing the seriousness of the business. (You can read about those in the other parts of this book).

One opportunity to lighten up is when we want to divide people into new groupings. Maybe it's to break up the usual cliques; maybe it's to make it easy for people to decide where to sit; or maybe we just want people to change seats in order to get a new perspective. I gave each person a Droodle. (Before the meeting, I had prepared six different Droodles. See Chapters 4 and 7 for examples.) Their task was to find all the others who had the same one, and then sit down together at a table. This meant that some people had to switch tables. I suggested they say goodbye to their dinner-mates, since they would now be sitting with new partners.

After settling in at their new places, their first task was to identify what the illustration was. This was very playful. Since there is no one right answer, everyone could participate without fear of being wrong. After about a minute of animated chatter, each Droodle was shown on the screen, and people guessed what it was. There was lots of laughter. And of course, it allowed me to make the point that we each see things differently, according to our own perspective and background of experiences.

Because everyone was relaxed at this point, I asked the participants to brainstorm together. "What are all the ways you can think of to make sure that the meetings you have with your staffs and with each other are really awful!" Playfully, yet with serious answers, they made their lists. The reason for this "back-door" approach became obvious: If we know what makes a poor meeting, we know what makes a good meeting. It's only a matter of having the skills, time, and interest to make good meetings happen.

For the rest of the meeting, we focused on additional opportunities to have a little fun: food, breaks, props, evaluations, presentations. (Examples can be found in other parts of this book, especially Chapters 6–10.) It's no wonder that at 7:30 p.m. so many people were still there. We were having a good time, laughing a lot, and eager for more. I believe that the only thing that caused us to end the meeting (at 8:00) was that everyone had to get home to prepare for the next day's meet-

ing. We all left in a very good mood, with many fresh ideas.

Ending on a Positive Note

Although you may have every intention of using a humorous approach to reduce tension, or build relationships, or maintain attention, or help to create a festive atmosphere, it *is* possible that your attempt at humor might fail. It might be misinterpreted. It might be seen as trivial. What can help to prevent that from happening?

First, make sure that you know something about your audience, whether it's a group of 5 or 100. And even if you don't know them, do something early on to find out something about them. Make an observation or ask a question.

Next, make sure that whatever you choose to do is in good taste, using the principles of **GIVE**: You want it to cause a **G**ood laugh, **I**nclude everyone, have no **V**ictim (unless it's yourself), and be **E**nergizing. It helps if you are comfortable yourself with the approach you use. If you are not, the group will sense it and might view your attempts to be lighthearted as phony. But if you truly have tried with all good intentions and your lighthearted attempt completely backfires, you can always smile, shrug your shoulders and say, "I tried."

☺   ☺   ☺

For a final smile, I leave you with a Pot Shot from Ashleigh Brilliant (see Figure 12.1).

Figure 12.1

Reprinted by permission of Ashleigh Brilliant. Copyright © 1987 by Ashleigh Brilliant.

Appendix

Questions and Topics to Aid Conversations

In this appendix you will find a number of questions and topics that help people get to know each other better in positive ways. These questions invite people to:

- remember (a first day on the job, a special holiday, a place they've lived);
- find similarities and differences (Who enjoys playing a sport that you don't like to play? Who likes one of the same movies you do? Who shares your childhood comic book hero?);
- perform (Who knows how to sing the theme song from "Gilligan's Island"?);
- share an idea (how to make work a little more fun);
- share knowledge (about a skill, talent, or resource);
- share an experience (a time you laughed really hard recently);
- share hopes and dreams (something you want to do some day); or

- share current involvement in an activity (something enjoyable you are doing these days).

Building Connections

The following topics and questions are especially good for groups where people don't know each other well but you want to encourage conversation that builds connections—what people have in common—on both a serious and lighthearted level.

These conversation aids can be used at association meetings; celebrations, such as bridal showers and weddings; parties; conferences; day-long retreats; learning events, such as Elderhostel, professional development sessions, and training programs; and in classrooms. These topics are especially good for the Secret Envelope activity described in Chapter 4.

- Tell something most people probably don't know about you.
- Sing or hum a song from your childhood.
- What is something for which you should be congratulated?
- What's an idea you would like to get before you leave this conference?
- Tell the story of how you got your name. If there is no story, make one up.
- Introduce yourself to someone the way your parents or a good friend would probably introduce you.
- What "first" did you experience this past year, either personally or professionally?
- "Hi, My name is NOT _____, but I'd like to try it for a day because . . . "
- How long have you been in this organization?
- Where are you from? Where were you born?
- What award do you deserve today?
- Who is a person from whom you can learn about lightening up?
- Who is a person who reminds you to lighten up?
- What is something about this organization that you're feeling very good about these days?
- Think of a word or phrase that makes you smile.
- What is your favorite number, and why?
- Report an achievement from childhood that made you feel wonderful.
- Imagine an expert on _____ is going to be coming through the door. What questions would you want to ask?

- What attracted you to this organization?
- When was the last time you laughed really hard?
- What is your favorite time of day, and why?
- What do you remember about coloring with crayons?
- Tell one thing you're really proud of.
- Who was one of your favorite childhood playmates, and why?
- What was one of your favorite toys as a child?
- What kinds of games did you play when you were in elementary school?
- What's the most embarrassing thing that has happened to you recently?
- Where is your favorite vacation spot?
- If you won a trip to go any place on this continent, where would you choose?
- What is your favorite dessert?
- If you could be any kind of animal, what would you be?
- What's one of the best books you've read in the past couple of years?
- What is one of your favorite Broadway musicals?
- What's your favorite color, and how does it make you feel?
- List all the questions you can think of that you'd like to ask others in this room.
- If you could ask only three questions to learn about another person, what would they be? (Now get into groups of two or three and ask each other.)

As the last item suggests, these topics can also be used for introducing twosomes, threesomes, or "moresomes" in any size group.

Treasure Hunts, Bingos, and Other Activities

These questions are particularly good for Treasure Hunts, Bingos, and other forms of "finding" someone in a group. They also can be used for creating smaller groups within the larger one (see Chapters 4 and 7).

Find someone who (or whose):

- is self-employed
- was not born in this state
- hand is the same size as yours
- eyes are same color as yours
- wears same shoe size as you do
- wears some item of clothing the same size as you do
- has no middle name
- was born in this city
- was not born in this city
- is personally acquainted with a celebrity
- regularly gets up before 6:00 a.m.
- drives a car that is more than 10 years old
- drives a motorcycle
- telephone number ends with the same digit as yours
- knows a good low-fat dessert recipe
- last name begins with the same letter as yours
- doesn't like vegetables
- can swim underwater
- has been to Disney World
- played a team sport in high school
- is active in a local charity organization
- remembers a clothing fad from high school
- used to hate a food as a child but likes it now

Introductions

Use questions from this list to discover interesting tidbits about the people in the group. They are especially good for Introductions, as described in Chapter 5.

- How long have you been in this organization?
- What do you remember about your first day on the job?
- What do you remember about your first meeting?
- Why are you here today?
- If you could rename your job, what would you call it, and why?
- What's something about you that we probably don't know?
- What's something you would like some help with?
- What could you teach to someone else?
- What special hobbies, talents, or interests do you have?

Appendix

B

Bingo and Treasure Hunt Variations

This appendix contains four activities for inviting a little laughter into your next meeting:

- Important Research! (Appendix B-1)
- Gee! I didn't know that . . . (Appendix B-2)
- Human Bingo (Appendix B-3)

- A HAPPY Human Treasure Hunt (Appendix B-4)

These activities reflect questions I have used in various types of meetings. They can—and should!—be amended, reordered, and otherwise adapted to the specific needs of your group or meeting (see Chapters 4 and 12).

B-1.
Important Research!

Directions: There are people in this room today who fit each of the following descriptions. **Use a name only once, and write it on the line.** See the facilitator when you've finished.

Find someone who:

1. Has a **birthday** in the same month as yours. _____

2. Likes prune juice! _____

3. Can tell you the **story** of his or her name. _____

4. Knows how to sing the theme song from "Gilligan's Island." _____

5. Deserves **Congratulations** for something—anything at all! _____

6. Was not born in (insert city). _____

7. Remembers his or her first part-time **job**. _____

8. **Has never met you**. (Be sure to introduce yourself!) _____

9. Will tell you what he or she thinks an "**inverse paranoid**" is. _____

10. Carries **something funny** in his or her purse, wallet, or briefcase. _____

11. Was active in a high school club or activity. _____

12. Can recite the **alphabet** backwards. _____

13. Has ever done something really "dumb." _____

14. Watched the same Saturday morning **cartoons** or listened to the same radio programs as you did when younger. _____

15. Currently plays, or used to play, a **musical instrument**. _____

16. Has a hole in his or her sock. _____

B-2.
Gee! I didn't know that . . .

Gee! I didn't know that . . .

1. _____ has a birthday in the same month as mine.

2. _____ likes prune juice!

3. _____ was born in the same state as I was.

4. _____ sings in a chorus and/or plays a muscial instrument.

5. _____ once won something.

6. _____ can recite the alphabet backwards.

7. _____ attended a fun meeting recently.

8. _____ did something "dumb" in the past week.

9. _____ knows the words to the "Brady Bunch" theme song.

10. _____ was active in a high school club or activity.

11. _____ has a little idiosyncracy.

12. _____ remembers an elementary school report card.

13. _____ listened to the same radio programs or watched the same cartoons as I did.

14. _____ found the typo on this page!

 **Amazing!**

B-3.

Human Bingo

Who wears a seatbelt at all times in the car?	Who does not eat breakfast?	Whose hand is the same size as yours?	Who has something to brag about?	
Whose first name begins with the same letter as yours?				
Whose birthday is in the same month as yours?	Who likes to play the same sport as you do?	Who has once made a bad mistake when working with a group?	Who was born in the same state as you?	
Who plays a musical instrument?				
Who can name the capitals of all 50 states?	**Your own name goes here.**	Who reads the newspaper from back to front?	Who has a new job as of this month?	
Who has an idea for a future (group name) project or meeting?				
Who knows a good ice-breaker?	Who was born in (insert city)	Whose eyes are the same color as yours?	Who has had the same job for more than 5 years? (or has worked at the same location)	
Who has an irrational fear?				
Who graduated from college with the same degree as yours? (same field of study)	Who got up before 5:30 a.m. today?	Who traveled more than 20 miles to be here?	Who can speak a foreign language?	
Who has never been outside the United States?				

B-4.

―――――――――――― *A HAPPY Human Treasure Hunt* ――――――――――――

Author's Note: I created the following activity as a way for meeting participants to get to know one another. But the activity also introduces the participants to *me*, because each of the items describes something about me. If you'd like your meeting participants to get to know you a little better while they meet each other, you can change the questions to reflect information about yourself. Or, if you don't want to personalize the activity that way, use these or other more general items.

The original activity had the following note at the top: "Do you want to know more about the author? Put her name in each of the blank spaces and you'll be right. Sorry, though: No prizes. Directions say, 'Use a name not more than twice.' Oh, well. . . . Happy to make your acquaintance!"

Directions: There are people in this room today who fit each of the following descriptions. Without using a name more than twice, fill in each line. Claim your prize when you've finished.

Find someone in the room who:

  1. was born in April _____

  2. likes prunes! _____

  3. can (and will) tell you the story of their name _____

  4. is not usually shy in a new group _____

  5. has three sons _____

  6. hates to wash floors _____

  7. doesn't mind ironing; actually finds it rather appealing _____

  8. was born and raised in Minneapolis _____

  9. is a grandparent _____

 10. carries something funny in his or her purse, wallet, or briefcase _____

 11. was active in a high school club or activity _____

 12. can recite the alphabet backwards _____

 13. has sewn on many Scout patches _____

 14. remembers listening to radio programs when younger _____

B-4.
————————————— *(continued)* —————————————

15. currently plays, or used to play, a musical instrument _____

16. gets up very early in the morning—and likes it! _____

17. worked at a summer camp _____

18. has been a junior high school teacher _____

19. loves to sing _____

20. has a nickname _____

21. belongs to a professional association _____

22. gets really crazy nervous about the weather and other things over which there's no control! _____

23. has been to a conference about humor _____

24. likes to walk for exercise, at least five to six times each week _____

25. loves good conversation _____

26. displays laughter-inviting items in the work place or at home _____

27. laughs hard at Mel Brooks and Carl Reiner doing "The 2000-Year-Old Man" _____

28. has taught at a University _____

29. knows how to do a magic trick _____

30. has worked in a factory _____

31. has naturally curly hair _____

32. has written a book _____

33. knows someone you know _____

34. has childhood memories of playing in the snow _____

35. wonders why some ready-made name tags say, "Hi, My Name is . . . "? (What do they think??? I'm going to write "My name isn't . . .????? Now *there's* an idea!)

    _____

Resources
Books About Meetings—and More

Decision-Making, Networking, Learning, and Celebration Meetings

Covey, S. (1989). *The seven habits of highly effective people*. New York: Fireside.

D'Amour, C. (1997). *Networking: The skill the schools forgot to teach*. Ann Arbor, MI: Jump Start Books.

Doyle, M., & Straus, D. (1993). *How to make meetings work: The new interaction method*. New York: Berkeley.

Haynes, M. (1988). *Effective meeting skills*. Los Altos, CA: Crisp.

Kemp, J. (1994). *Moving meetings*. Burr Ridge, IL: Irwin Professional Publishing.

Lippitt, R., Schindler-Rainman, E., & Cole, J. (1977). *Taking your meetings out of the doldrums*. La Jolla, CA: University Associates.

Pike, R. (1994). *Creative training techniques handbook*. Minneapolis, MN: Lakewood.

Scannell, E., & Newstrom, J. W. (1994). *Even more games trainers play*. New York: McGraw-Hill.

Silva, K. (1994). *Meetings that work*. Burr Ridge, IL: Irwin Professional Publishing.

Tropman, J. (1996). *Making meetings work: Achieving high quality group decisions*. Thousand Oaks, CA: Sage Publications

The Power of Humor, Laughter, and Fun

Antion, T. (1997). *Wake 'em up: How to use humor and other professional techniques to create alarmingly good business presentations*. Landover Hills, MD: Anchor Publishing.

Blumenfeld, E., & Alpern, L. (1994). *Humor at work*. Atlanta, GA: Peachtree.

Cousins, N. (1979). *Anatomy of an illness as perceived by the patient*. New York: Norton.

Garland, R. (1991). *Making work fun*. San Diego, CA: Shamrock.

Goodman, J. (1983). How to get more smileage out of your life. In P. McGhee & J. Goldstein (Eds.), *Handbook of humor research. Vol. II. Applied studies* (pp. 1–21). New York: Springer-Verlag.

Goodman, J. (1991). The magic of humor: Laughing all the way to the learning bank. *Laughing Matters, 1*(1).

Goodman, J. (1995). *Laffirmations: 1,001 ways to add humor to your life and work*. Deerfield Beach, FL: Health Communications.

Helitzer, M. (1987). *Comedy writing secrets: How to think funny, write funny, act funny, and get paid for it*. Cincinnati, OH: Writer's Digest Books.

Hoff, R. (1988). *I can see you naked: A fearless guide to making great presentations*. Kansas City, MO: Andrews and McMeel.

Klein, A. (1989). *The healing power of humor.* Los Angeles: Jeremy Tarcher.

Kushner, M. (1990). *The light touch: How to use humor for business success.* New York: Simon and Schuster.

Loomans, D., & Kolberg, K. (1993). *The laughing classroom: Everyone's guide to teaching with humor and play.* Tiburon, CA: H. J. Kramer.

McGhee, P., & Goldstein, J. (1983). *Handbook of humor research* (Vols I & II). New York: Springer-Verlag.

Metcalf, C. W., & Felible, R. (1992). *Lighten up: Survival skills for people under pressure.* Reading, MA: Addison-Wesley.

Paulson, T. (1989). *Making humor work: Take your job seriously and yourself lightly.* Los Altos, CA: Crisp.

Peter, L., & Dana, B. (1982). *The laughter prescription.* New York: Ballantine.

Pike, R. (1996, November). The power of the interactive keynote. *Professional Speaker 5*(3), 12–14.

Quereau, T., & Zimmermann, T. (1993). *The new game plan for recovery: Rediscovering the positive power of play.* New York: Ballantine.

Thurston, C., & Lundberg, E. (1992). *If they're laughing, they're not killing each other.* Fort Collins, CO: Cottonwood Press.

Weinstein, M., & Goodman, J. (1980). *Playfair: Everybody's guide to noncompetitive play.* San Luis Obispo, CA: Impact Publishers.

Wilson, S. (1992). *The art of mixing work and play: Pwloaryk.* Columbus, OH: Applied Humor Systems.

For Fun and Inspiration

Brilliant, A. (1978). *I may not be totally perfect, but parts of me are excellent.* Santa Barbara, CA: Woodbridge Press.

Brilliant, A. (1980). *I have abandoned my search for truth and am now looking for a good fantasy.* Santa Barbara, CA: Woodbridge Press.

Brilliant, A. (1981). *Appreciate me now and avoid the rush.* Santa Barbara, CA: Woodbridge Press.

Brilliant, A. (1984). *I feel much better now that I've given up hope.* Santa Barbara, CA: Woodbridge Press.

Brilliant, A. (1985). *All I want is a warm bed and a kind word and unlimited power.* Santa Barbara, CA: Woodbridge Press.

Brilliant, A. (1987). *I try to take one day at a time, but sometimes several days attack me at once.* Santa Barbara, CA: Woodbridge Press.

Brilliant, A. (1990). *We've been through so much together, and most of it was your fault.* Santa Barbara, CA: Woodbridge Press.

Brilliant, A. (1994). *I want to reach your mind . . . where is it currently located?* Santa Barbara, CA: Woodbridge Press.

Byrne, R. (1988). *1,911 best things anybody ever said.* New York: Fawcett Columbine.

Charles, C. L. (1995) *Stick to it! The power of positive persistence.* Lansing, MI: Yes! Press.

Klein, A. (1991). *Quotations to cheer you up when the world is getting you down.* New York: Sterling Publishing Co.

MAD. (1997). *The half-wit and wisdom of Alfred E. Neuman. Classic pearls of idiocy.* New York: Warner Books, Inc.

Price, R. (1992). *Classic droodles.* Los Angeles: Price Stern Sloan, Inc.

Wilson, S. (1990). *Eat dessert first: A wonderful collection of quotes and quips about the amazing powers of joy, playfulness, laughter, humor.* Pickerington, OH: Advocate Publishing Group.

Catalogs

HUMOResources. The HUMOR Project, Inc., 480 Broadway, Suite 210, Saratoga Springs, NY 12866-2288. Phone: 518-587-8770.

Oriental Trading Company. P.O. Box 3407, Omaha, NE 68103. Phone: 1-800-228-2199.

Spirit Lifters Co. P.O. Box 601, Front Royal, VA 22630. Phone: 540-635-5829. (They're the creators of "Happy Rocks.")

Periodicals

Laughing Matters. Joel Goodman, Editor. Quarterly publication of The HUMOR Project since 1981. 480 Broadway, Suite 210, Saratoga Springs, NY 12866-2288.

Professional Speaker. Journal of the National Speakers Association. 1500 S. Priest Dr., Tempe, AZ 85281.

Index

About the Author

Sheila Feigelson makes meetings fun while getting things done.

Early in her career as an educator, Feigelson recognized the power of humor to create a motivating and stimulating classroom climate. Over the past 25 years, as consultant, speaker, and workshop leader, she has helped clients and audiences put their natural sense of humor and fun to work, resulting in more enjoyable and productive meetings.

Feigelson has taught junior high school and served as student-teaching supervisor, as well as an instructor, at The University of Michigan. As a "Humor Consultant," Feigelson has been a featured speaker and facilitator at numerous national and regional conferences. Among them are the International Conference on the Positive Power of Humor and Creativity, the National Association of

Girl Scout Executive Staff, Young Presidents Organization, and Elderhostel.

A native of Minneapolis, the author is a graduate of the University of Minnesota and holds a Ph.D. in education from The University of Michigan. She is a member of the National Speakers Association and is active in other professional and civic groups.

She and her husband live in Ann Arbor. They are the proud parents of three sons and their growing families.

For further information about speaking and consulting services, contact the author at:

Happy Associates
P.O. Box 7262
Ann Arbor, MI 48107
Telephone: 734-662-1996
E-Mail: HappyF@aol.com

☺   ☺   ☺